MY APOLOGETICS DINNER PARTY

A REAL-LIFE SOCRATIC DIALOGUE

LOUIS MARKOS

An imprint of InterVarsity Press
Downers Grove, Illinois

InterVarsity Press
P.O. Box 1400 | Downers Grove, IL 60515-1426
ivpress.com | email@ivpress.com

InterVarsity Press® is the publishing division of InterVarsity Christian Fellowship/USA®. For more information, visit intervarsity.org.

Cover design: Gearbox with Faceout Studio
Interior design: Jeanna Wiggins
Images: © Alarcon Studios / iStock via Getty Images

ISBN 978-1-5140-1444-8 (print) | ISBN 978-1-5140-1445-5 (digital)

Printed in the United States of America ♾

Library of Congress Cataloging-in-Publication Data
A catalog record for this book is available from the Library of Congress.

33 32 31 30 29 28 27 26 | 13 12 11 10 9 8 7 6 5 4 3 2 1

"This is a dinner party to savor and remember. Through a multi-course Socratic dialogue with Christians, skeptics, and adherents of other faiths, Louis Markos presents the gospel in a way that is faithful yet fresh and accessible for the twenty-first century."

Nadya Williams, books editor at *Mere Orthodoxy* and author of *Mothers, Children, and the Body Politic*

"A tough challenge faced by all Christians is how to explain and defend their convictions—how to transform their knowledge about God into conversations with real people. They need models. That's what Louis Markos gives us in this book—a wealth of models based on real conversations with people from many different countries and walks of life. Read it to hone your skills of communication with the people in your life."

Nancy Pearcey, professor and scholar in residence at Houston Christian University and author of *Total Truth* and *Love Thy Body*

"The delivery of Christian apologetics is happily moving from philosophical texts to conversational encounters. Cafés, podcasts, radio programs, and informal centers are proving to be safe places for hearing the gospel. Louis Markos's Thanksgiving potluck is Exhibit A for this kind of encounter. Although the Christian 'wins,' the skeptic represented in these dialogues comes across as an authentic person. These questions and answers are tried and true. The setting, however, is relatively original. If this is the future for apologetics dialogues, the future is bright."

William Edgar, professor emeritus of apologetics at Westminster Theological Seminary

"*My Apologetics Dinner Party* serves us two things even more delicious than the dinner: an extended Socratic dialogue and a popular but persuasive apologetic for the crucial and controversial claims of *Mere Christianity* à la C. S. Lewis. Rarely has profundity been so clear and so much fun."

Peter Kreeft, professor of philosophy at Boston College and author of *Between Heaven and Hell* and *The Best Things in Life*

THIS BOOK IS DEDICATED TO

Houston International Christian Fellowship (HICF)

and to Bobby and Martha Mathew,

who helped found it over forty years ago.

May its ministry continue for another forty years!

CONTENTS

INTRODUCTION

SETTING THE TABLE

HAD I THE SLIGHTEST INKLING OF WHAT an exhausting and Herculean but thoroughly stimulating labor this Thanksgiving would turn out to be, I would have eaten my dinner *before* the guests arrived!

For many years, I had been hosting an international Thanksgiving potluck at my home. Since I didn't know until the day itself who would come or what they would bring, each meal proved to be a one-of-a-kind experience. I never knew what countries or faith traditions would be represented. Previous dinners had brought Christian believers of all denominations, as well as people with a Christian upbringing who were questioning various aspects of their faith. Followers of Judaism, Islam, Hinduism, and Buddhism, not to mention deists, skeptics, atheists, and New Agers, had all attended as well.

But never before had so many come and from such radically diverse nations, backgrounds, and faith journeys. It was truly invigorating, and made me feel thankful that I lived in a country where such a multiethnic, religiously pluralistic meeting was possible, where conversations could range and rage across a multitude of topics without anyone drawing their swords or reaching for their guns or feeling the need to conceal their deepest doubts and most perplexing questions.

My job that day was not so much to answer every question with airtight logic and irrefutable proofs as to clarify what Christians actually *do* believe, to distinguish the myth from the history, the rumors from the facts, the urban legends from the true stories.

Well, that's what I would end up doing for most of the evening, but it's not where I began. All I could think of when the clock struck three was that the person bringing the turkey had not yet arrived. This was somewhat problematic, given that the dinner was scheduled to begin at two o'clock! Since I have learned through my work with internationals that punctuality is an American virtue—or hangup—not shared by most people outside northern Europe, I didn't take it personally. Still, I had to do something to keep my hungry guests entertained while we waited for the entrée. The fact that my wife was out of town visiting relatives, leaving me in sole charge of the festivities, merely added another layer of butterflies to my stomach.

Luckily, my daughter, Stacey, happens to be a vocal performance major at my university who possesses a wonderfully clear and pure soprano voice. In order to divert attention away from growling stomachs, I lifted up my right hand and announced, with barely concealed pride, that my daughter would perform "Silent Night" for us. In typical fatherly fashion, I didn't consult her before making the offer, but then she was used to such things. I felt quite sure she wouldn't let us down . . . and she didn't.

While I played the three-chord tune on my eighty-eight-year-old piano, Stacey sang the first stanza with a depth of feeling that caused a hush to fall over the room:

> Silent night! Holy night!
> All is calm, all is bright
> Round yon Virgin Mother and Child
> Holy Infant so tender and mild
> Sleep in heavenly peace!
> Sleep in heavenly peace!

As she sang the last word, I felt all my anxieties melt away. I was not the only person in the room who felt transported, for a brief, shimmering moment, to the manger. *Yes*, I thought to myself, *this is going to be a peaceful Thanksgiving indeed.*

With a grand flourish, I swiveled around on my piano bench to face my guests, all of whom were sitting in a large circle in my den. Because of the frequent parties and Bible studies I hosted at my home, I had purchased four large leather couches, one for each side of the den. The couches alone could accommodate fourteen guests, but I had interspersed half a dozen free-standing chairs in the empty spaces between the couches to allow for an even larger group.

On the bench to my immediate left, Bobby, his wife, Martha, and their son, David, sat together. They were longtime members of the fellowship; in fact, Bobby and Martha had started the group some thirty years earlier. To their left sat two of my former students, an Egyptian American named Anthony and an Indian American named Sita.

To their left sat an Iranian man named Reza and a Chinese woman named Elaine. In the fourth couch, which was positioned directly to my left, Stacey sat alone, for she was saving a seat for her brother, Alex. To complete the group, a ninety-five-year-old man named Stewart sat in a large dining room chair with wooden arms that I had moved into the den to help support his back.

As I surveyed the room, enjoying the smiles on the faces of those who had been blessed by my daughter's singing, I noticed that Anthony looked troubled. He had taken one of my English classes as an elective four years earlier and had shown himself to be an inquisitive but respectful young man. He had grown up in a Christian home to parents who had immigrated to Houston from Egypt, but he had always struggled with the issue of miracles.

I remember he once shared with me a story about an icon in his Coptic Orthodox church of the Virgin Mary that had started weeping. Apparently, when other icons were placed next to it, they would start weeping as well. He didn't ridicule these claims—like most of my Egyptian students, he was a polite young man with an ingrained respect for tradition and authority—but I could tell that he was troubled by the thought that something could happen for which he could find no natural, scientific explanation.

Ever since he had started his studies at the Baylor School of Medicine, his doubts about the miraculous had increased. He simply couldn't square what he read in the Bible with what he had learned in school about the human body and the laws of nature.

"Anthony," I said, "something seems to be worrying you."

"It is, Dr. Markos," he said, "but I feel embarrassed to say it in this group."

"Please don't be embarrassed," I replied, "We're all friends here, and no question is ever off the table."

"All right, but remember that I warned you. It's about the Christmas carol your daughter just sang. It was beautiful, but there's a phrase in it that bothers me."

"What phrase is that?"

"'Virgin Mother.' Isn't that an oxymoron?"

Well, well, I thought to myself, *this is going to be an interesting Thanksgiving.*

FIRST COURSE

PREDINNER IN THE DEN

1

ARE MIRACLES POSSIBLE?

"ANTHONY," I ASKED, taking a deep breath and praying that my smile looked genuine, "why do you say that 'Virgin Mother' is an oxymoron?"

"Everybody knows that a woman can't give birth to a child unless she has sex with a man. That's simple science. If the people back in Jesus' day thought his mother was a virgin, that was only because they didn't understand how procreation works."

"If you mean they did not know about sperm and eggs, then you are right. But tell me this. When Mary told Joseph that she was pregnant by the Holy Spirit, how did Joseph react?"

"He was upset and was prepared to divorce her in secret?"

"Why did he want to divorce her?"

"Because he thought that she had been unfaithful?"

"Why did he think that?"

"Well, she was pregnant, and Joseph knew he had not had sex with her. That meant she must have slept with another man."

"Ah, so what you are telling me, Anthony, is that Joseph, though he knew nothing about sperm and eggs, was well aware that women don't get pregnant if they haven't had sex?"

"Of course he knew that. . . . I mean . . . well . . . oh my."

"Don't worry, Anthony, I can't tell you how many times I have heard highly educated professors say that the people of the past believed in miracles only because they were ignorant of the laws of nature. I hope you see now the flaw in that argument. The only way a person can *recognize* that a miracle like the virgin birth has occurred is if he is fully aware of the way things normally work in nature.

"When Jesus raised Lazarus from the dead after he had been in the tomb for four days, the crowd was shocked and terrified. They reacted that way because they all knew that dead people don't walk out of graves. And the same goes for blind men being able to see and lame men being able to walk. If they did not know that the dead, the blind, and the lame don't suddenly wake, see, and walk, they wouldn't have thought it miraculous, or even out of the ordinary, when they did.

"Stacey," I said, turning to my daughter, "do you remember the enchanted pig?"

The moment I said those words, she broke into laughter, causing everyone else to wonder what could possibly be so funny about a pig, enchanted or otherwise.

"When my kids were young," I explained, "I read them fairy stories from the red and blue fairy books of Andrew Lang. One of them concerned an enchanted pig that came to the royal court to ask for the hand of the princess. Stacey, please tell everyone what the king said to the pig after he finished making his suit."

"Pig," she said in a deep voice, "I am surprised that you speak so eloquently." And then she started laughing again.

"You see," I continued, knowing that once my daughter started laughing, it was difficult to get her to stop, "the king was not surprised that the pig *spoke*, only that it spoke eloquently."

As Stacey continued to laugh, Anthony, along with most of the guests, stared at her and me with a blank expression.

"In our world," I said, "we would all be shocked if a pig began to speak. That is because we live in a world in which animals do not possess the gift of speech. But in the realms of fairy, animals are just as likely to talk as people, and that's why the king doesn't bat an eye when the pig talks to him. He is surprised only that so lowly an animal should have mastered the high language of the court.

"Or, to bring things back to our world, suppose we all went outside on the front lawn, and I asked Anthony to walk over to the sidewalk and jump as high as he could. If you did that, Anthony, what would happen?"

"I'd jump up and immediately come back down."

"Exactly, because we live in a world in which gravity draws things downward.

"Would that same rule hold for a person living in the Middle Ages or the time of Christ or the golden age of Greece?"

"Yes."

"But what if you jumped, Anthony, and, rather than immediately come back down, you floated away into the sky?"

"That's impossible—unless I were performing a magic trick with hidden wires."

"Of course it is, but if you did float away without the use of ropes or wires, would you call that a miracle? Wouldn't you all call that a miracle?"

Anthony, along with all the other guests, nodded his head.

"And what about the medievals or early Christians or ancient Athenians who saw one of their friends float away? Would they not recognize it as a miracle as well, despite the fact that they never heard the word *gravity*?"

"Yes. You don't need to know the formula for gravity to know that it works."

"But what if we moved the whole party to the surface of the moon. If you jumped on the moon and floated away, would that be a miracle."

"No, because there is less gravity on the moon."

"So, if we can sum up, people recognize that a miracle has occurred only if they know that a natural law has been violated, and they know if it has been violated only if they know that such laws exist. And the people of the past knew just as well as we do that human beings don't float away, that people don't come back from the dead, and that women don't get pregnant if they have not slept with a man."

I could tell by the looks on the faces of my hungry guests that all of them had understood the argument and that most of them had found it reasonable, but Anthony still looked unconvinced. As I saw the skepticism in his eyes, I said a silent prayer that the turkey would arrive and get me off the hook, but I was to have no such luck.

"All right," said Anthony, and then paused to let the words coalesce in his head, "I'll concede that the people of Jesus' day knew the laws of nature, even if they didn't have scientific terminology to express it. The real problem is not that they knew about the laws of nature but that they believed, incorrectly, that those laws could be broken at will. Hasn't modern science proved that the laws of nature cannot be broken?"

"Good point, Anthony. I see exactly where you're coming from. Modern skeptics are right when they say that the laws of nature can't be broken."

"Wait a minute, are you agreeing with me that miracles are impossible?"

"If miracles did in fact break the laws of nature, then I would agree with you. But I don't agree that they do. Miracles don't break the laws; they suspend them."

"What's the difference?"

By the looks on the faces of those around me, I could tell that Anthony's point about the laws of nature being unbreakable had engaged them enough to take their minds off dinner. As two dozen eyes fell on me, I looked at my bookshelf in hopes of locating a delicate Chinese vase that one of my students had once given me as a present. Spying it in the top corner by my books of mythology, I went over to the shelf and plucked it down. Then, with the vase in my right hand, I moved to the center of the den.

"Anthony," I asked, lifting up my right hand as high as it would go, "What would happen to this vase if I let it go?"

"It would fall to the ground and shatter."

"Exactly. We are back to the unbreakable law of gravity. But watch this."

As everyone in the room, especially Elaine, gasped with horror, I opened my hand and let the vase fall. Another second and it would have smashed to pieces, but the crash never came. Before the vase could hit the ground, my left hand swooped across and caught it mid-fall.

"OK, Anthony," I said with a smile, "did I just break the law of gravity."

"No."

"Then what happened?"

"You altered the course of the vase by catching it with your left hand."

"In other words, I suspended the natural course of gravity by adding in a new factor. What will happen if I open my left hand?"

"Gravity will take over again, and the vase will break."

"Do you see now the difference between breaking and suspending the laws of gravity? Increasingly since Isaac Newton, modern scientists and philosophers have come to view our universe as a giant billiard table run by fixed laws of motion. If you hit a ball with your cue stick with such and such force and at such and such an angle, and if there is no friction on the table, the ball must follow a certain course."

"But isn't that true? Isn't that how the laws of nature work?"

"Yes, they do. But what would happen if, the second after you hit the ball, two hands reached out and shook the table?"

"The course of the ball would follow an unpredictable pattern."

"Yes, because the intervention of those two hands suspended but didn't break the physical laws of motion."

"I agree, but I don't see what that has to do with miracles like the virgin birth."

"A miracle takes place when the hand of God reaches into our physical world and suspends, for a moment, the natural course of the laws that run it. But once he pulls his hand back, the normal laws of nature resume."

"But you can't bring someone back to life after he's died."

"Anthony, the Gospels record three miracles where Jesus raised someone from the dead. All three of those people that he brought back to life eventually died, just as all those he healed from sickness eventually got sick again."

"But what about the virgin birth?"

"The Bible tells us that the Holy Spirit overshadowed Mary and that she conceived and became pregnant (Lk 1:30-35). Although Luke's Gospel provides no details on the mechanics of how this miracle occurred, there is one thing that is clear."

"What's that?"

"Mary did not give birth to Jesus two days later. After Mary was found to be with child by the Holy Spirit, she carried the child for nine months and delivered him in the natural manner that all babies have been delivered since Cain and Abel.

"The difference between the early and medieval Christians and us is not that we think the laws of nature are inviolable and they did not, but that they were open, while we are not, to the possibility of the supernatural breaking in to the natural world."

For a second a hush fell over the group, rather like the hush that fell after Stacey sang "Silent Night." All of us, myself included, were feeling a quiet sense of awe at the thought that our natural world might not after all be fixed, static, and closed.

But I could tell that something was still bothering Anthony.

"Go ahead, Anthony," I said. "Tell us what's on your mind."

"I'm not sure how to say it, but there's something else about miracles that just doesn't sit right with me. I mean, if God created the world and established the laws of nature, then why would he keep meddling with them? Doesn't that seem to you, well, rather undignified, even a bit sloppy?"

"I see what you mean. Miracles seem to break the set order and rhythm of the cosmos, and as such suggest that God is a poor playwright who has lost control of the story he is telling. Is that what you're trying to say?"

"Yes."

"OK, then, let's explore the analogy a bit further. Tell me, Anthony, who would you say is the greatest playwright who ever lived?"

"That's easy. Shakespeare."

"I don't think anyone would disagree with that answer, but did you know that during the Enlightenment, what in England we call the Age of Reason, Shakespeare was considered to be a rather sloppy craftsman?"

"That sounds crazy."

"It does to us, but in the eighteenth century, though they recognized the genius of Shakespeare's soliloquies, critics felt that the overall design of his plays was flawed. Critics such as Samuel Johnson expected plays to follow the strict rules of decorum laid down by Aristotle and Horace, and, because Shakespeare didn't think twice about breaking those rules, they felt he was an erratic genius at best."

"What happened to change people's minds about Shakespeare?"

"The Romantic poet and critic Samuel Taylor Coleridge is what happened."

"Isn't he the one who wrote *The Rime of the Ancient Mariner*?"

"The same. He decided to take a second look at Shakespeare's plays. When he did, he discovered a deeper, more organic unity. True, Shakespeare broke the surface rules, but that is only because his grasp of the whole was fuller and richer. Just as every acorn contains within it the blueprint for an oak forest, so, we now know, each of our microscopic cells contains the DNA code that sets the pattern for every part of our body.

"Remember in my class, Anthony, when you had to choose one image or metaphor from *Hamlet* and trace its use across the full length of the play?"

"I remember that well. It turned out to be the best essay I wrote during my four years at Houston Christian."

"It *was* a good paper, Anthony. That's because you understood that *Hamlet* is like a complex tapestry made up of a thousand crisscrossing threads. The metaphor you chose to analyze—poison, if memory serves—was one of those threads. It surfaces in act one, then goes dormant, then remerges, always in a slightly different way. The pattern is there in the play, but you don't realize it until you study it more closely."

"Yes, that's true," said Anthony, looking enthusiastically at the other guests. "When I read the play again in a more focused manner, the pattern magically emerged. Before I did that, it was invisible. It was there all along, but I didn't *see* it."

"That's because you didn't yet have eyes to see it."

"Or ears to hear it," chimed in Stacey.

"That's right, Stacey!" I said with fatherly pride. "Many of us learned in Sunday school that Jesus taught in parables so that everyone would understand him. But that's not what Jesus said. He said that he taught in parables so that only those who had eyes to see and ears to hear would understand (Mk 4:10-12).

"Can anyone tell me what message John the Baptist sent to Jesus after Herod Antipas put John in prison?"

As Bible questions go, that was a tough one, and it was understandably followed by about twenty seconds of silence. Finally, however, an answer did come, and from just the place I expected it to.

David had been a student of mine almost ten years earlier. In fact, he was the very person who had ushered me in to the international Christian fellowship group that was sponsoring the Thanksgiving potluck. His father, who had been born in India, and his mother, who had been born in Mexico, had started the group before he was born.

My entry into the group began when David, a senior at the time taking my class on *The Chronicles of Narnia*, invited me to speak for one of their Saturday night meetings. I immediately agreed, only to discover a few days before the scheduled meeting that I couldn't follow through on my commitment because I'm deathly allergic to cats and dogs, and David's family, as it turned out, had a dog.

I was just about to email him my regrets when an idea struck me out of the blue: Why not move the fellowship to my home on Saturday? Well, that's exactly what we did, and the rest, as they say, is history. The group has been meeting at my house once a month ever since—and I wouldn't give up a single meeting!

Even as a senior, David was a powerful evangelist with a strong knowledge of the Bible; the intervening years had only strengthened that knowledge and sharpened his love for Christ, the gospel, and the Word of God.

"John the Baptist," he said, "had two of his disciples go to Jesus and ask him whether he was the Messiah promised by God or whether he should wait for someone else (Lk 7:19)."

"Exactly," I said with a smile, for a teacher is always pleased when his student gets an answer right, even if he hasn't taught him for eight years, "though I must admit I'm shocked that John would ask such a question. After all, John was the one God used to identify Jesus as the Son of God (Jn 1:32-34) and thus initiate his ministry.

"Still, John was confused and worried and wanted to get a straight answer from the lips of Jesus himself. Did Jesus give him the straight yes he was looking for?"

"Yes and no," said David. "He didn't give a direct yes. Rather, he told John's disciples to report back to John and tell him what was happening in Galilee: that the blind were seeing, the lame walking, the deaf hearing, the lepers being cleansed, the dead being raised, and the good news being preached to the poor (Lk 7:22-23)."

"Was Jesus being evasive?"

"No, he was offering up those miracles as a sign that he was the Messiah."

"Thanks, David," I said and then turned back to Anthony. "Anthony, do you see the point of this story? Miracles are not random, haphazard events that strike the earth like meteors that have fallen out of their orbit. They are purposeful. In the Old Testament, they were signs of God's presence in the history of Israel, particularly when he led them out of slavery in Egypt, when he gave them the law of Moses, and when he spoke through the judges and prophets to get them back on track after they had strayed from the law.

"In the New Testament, they point to an amazing fact: that the God who created the world entered in to the world and became a man. They further attest to the good news that God in Christ has defeated sin and death and that he is building his church through the disciples. And miracles continue today, for God's church is always dying and being reborn, just like its founder. Miracles don't just *do* something; they *mean* something. They mean that God's Spirit is working in the world.

"Anthony, the modern scientific mind takes for granted that miracles are aberrations, faulty stitches in the weave of nature, just as Samuel Johnson thought Shakespeare's deviations from dramatic decorum rendered his plays flawed and imperfect. But if the Bible is right, then our world is fallen and in a state of decay. What if the miracle is not a break or a flaw in the story but a brief, tantalizing moment during which the original order is restored? Maybe miracles offer an all-too-brief glimpse into the way things were meant to be. When the Creator himself enters in to his creation, how else should that creation respond?"

"But water simply doesn't turn into wine," said Anthony, "and you can't feed five thousand men with five loaves of bread and two fish."

"Stacey," I said, "could you please go in my study and get my copy of *Miracles* by C. S. Lewis?" As my ever-helpful daughter went in search of the book, I summed up for Anthony and the other guests what Lewis had to say about Jesus' first miracle, when he turned six stone jars filled with water into six jugs of the finest wine to provide convivial cheer for those attending a wedding at Cana in Galilee (Jn 2:1-11).

"Every day, Lewis explains, water turns into wine, but the process is very slow and happens in secret. But when Jesus shows up and does it in a flash, the veil is lifted, and we get to see the miracle that has been going on for millennia. The same goes for the feeding of the five thousand (Mk 6:30-44). Every day, some wheat becomes much wheat, and a few fish become many fish, but we don't notice the miracle. Until Jesus does it in a flash, and we suddenly recognize the fecundity the Creator put into his creation."

"Our eyes are opened," said Anthony with a slow nod of his head.

"Yes. We recognize not only that what we call nature was fashioned by the hand of a personal Creator but that that Creator is among us."

At just that moment, Stacey arrived with book in hand. "Here it is, Dad. I've opened it to the page I think you have in mind."

"Well done, daughter! Here is what Lewis writes in chapter fifteen: 'Every year, as part of the Natural order, God makes wine. He does so by creating a vegetable organism that can turn water, soil, and sunlight into a juice which will, under proper conditions, become wine. Thus, in a certain sense, He constantly turns water into wine, for wine, like all drinks, is but water modified. Once, and in one year only, God, now incarnate, short circuits the process: makes wine in a moment; uses earthenware jars instead of vegetable fibres to hold the water. But uses them to do what He is always doing. The miracle consists in the short cut; but the event to which it leads is the usual one.'

"Anthony, do you remember in class when we read Ovid's *Metamorphoses*?"

"How could I forget? People turning into bears and birds and trees and stones! Sometimes they even turn into rivers or flowers or stars. I really enjoyed that book."

"But would you have enjoyed it if you thought that those things might happen?"

"Of course not! I would be terrified if I thought it was even remotely possible that such things might happen to me or someone I know."

"If the 'miracles' in Ovid were true, what would that tell you about the world in which we live?"

"That it's run by arbitrary gods who help us to become heroes or transform us into animals depending on their mood."

"Did you know that Ovid wrote his *Metamorphoses* about fifty years before the Gospel of Mark? Ovid's life overlaps with that of Jesus."

"Really? But the miracles of Jesus are radically different from those in Ovid."

"How so? Can you explain the difference?"

"I would say that those in Ovid are performed by random, capricious gods who seem to care nothing for the people whose lives they interfere with, while those in Mark are performed by a good, moral God who wants to help and heal humanity."

"Well put, Anthony. Would you say, then, that in the miracles recorded in the Gospels, we see the hand of a loving God who works with and through his creation rather than violating and disrupting its laws?"

"Yes, I think that's a fair statement. The miracles in the Bible really are different from those we read about in Greek and Roman mythology. Ovid's miracles break the laws of nature, while those in the Bible work through them."

"Yes, just as Jesus the teacher did not break the Mosaic law but fulfilled it (Mt 5:17), so Jesus the miracle worker did not break the laws of nature but fulfilled them. As Lewis himself reminds us in the same chapter I just read from, when God created the first man, Adam, he did it directly, bypassing what would become the normal route of procreation. Just so, when he created the second Adam, the perfect Man, Jesus, he also bypassed the normal route so that Mary conceived by the Holy Spirit. The virgin birth does not violate the scientific laws of procreation; it reveals that the original seed came from God and that he, not our parents, is the real author of human life."

When I could see from Anthony's body language that he was a bit more comfortable now with the idea of a Virgin Mother, I turned my attention to the group as a whole and said: "Yes, the virgin birth is a difficult thing to bend one's mind around, but it is not the greatest miracle in Christianity. The virgin birth, as amazing as it is, is merely the vehicle that brought about the greatest miracle of all: the incarnation, that Jesus of Nazareth was fully man and fully God."

"Wait a minute," said a voice to my left, "those two miracles don't have to go together. In my religion, we accept and teach the virgin birth, but we reject what you call the incarnation. Our book teaches us that Jesus was a prophet born of a virgin but that he was not the Son of God."

This would be a most opportune time for that turkey to arrive, I thought to myself, but the front door remained stubbornly shut. This question too would need to be wrestled with.

2

WHO DID JESUS CLAIM TO BE?

AMERICAN CHRISTIANS WHO HAVE NEVER READ the Qur'an are generally shocked to learn that Muhammad believed and taught that Mary was a virgin when she gave birth to Jesus. Still, despite accepting that miracle, Muhammad categorically denied the most vital, nonnegotiable of all Christian doctrines: that Jesus was the one-and-only God-man, 100 percent human and 100 percent divine.

In fact, to drive that point home, there is a scene in the Qur'an in which the newborn Jesus speaks to those around him and proclaims that he is not the Son of God, only his servant and prophet (sura 19, verses 27-36). Again and again, the Qur'an emphasizes that God has no partners of any kind, especially no wife or son (4:171-73; 5:116; 6:100-103; 72:3). Indeed, the central proclamation of Christianity, that God is a Trinity (one God but three persons: Father, Son, and Holy Spirit) and that the Second Person of that Trinity was fully God and fully man, was rejected by Muhammad and his followers.

Given that aspect of Islam, I wasn't at all surprised when Reza (pronounced RAY-zah), a middle-aged engineer from Iran, said that the Qur'an accepted the virgin birth but rejected the incarnation. He was in fact absolutely correct.

This was only the third time Reza had been to my home. He had mostly grown up in America, for he was quite young when his parents fled Iran for Texas during the takeover by the Ayatollah Khomeini. He was a Shia

Muslim who knew his Qur'an well, but, like many Iranian Muslims, he had never forgotten that Persia had had her own great prophet, Zoroaster. He was an educated, open-minded man who liked to study different religions and who was not afraid to ask questions. As you can imagine, I liked him immediately. Although twenty-five hundred years ago, my Greek ancestors had fought against his Persian ancestors in a great war, today in America, especially on Thanksgiving, we could meet and break bread together as friends.

"Reza," I said after pausing to collect my thoughts, "you are right to say that the Qur'an says that God has no Son. But let me ask you this question. What does the Qur'an have to say about the Bible? Do Muslims accept the Bible as authoritative scripture?"

"Yes and no," he replied. "Although Muslims do not accept the full Bible, the Qur'an does say that God sent the Torah and the Gospel (3:2-4). That is why we consider Jews and Christians to be people of the Book."

"So, as a Muslim, you believe that the Five Books of Moses and the Four Gospels (Matthew, Mark, Luke, and John) constitute divine revelation."

"Yes."

"Reza, let me begin by saying something you may find shocking. Although Muhammad taught that Jesus was a prophet but not the Son of God, a position shared by many Jews, there are a large number of people who call themselves Christians who believe the same thing. That is to say, they respect Jesus as a great rabbi or teacher, but they do not believe that he was the Son of God or even that he was born of a virgin."

"That is surprising."

"It is indeed, and it raises an important question for all people of all religions, even those who grew up in a Christian home."

"What question is that?"

"Did Jesus actually claim to be the Son of God, or is that just something later Christians invented?"

"I agree that that is a very important question."

"Would you be willing to consider the question with me by looking at some of Jesus' actual words?"

"I would!"

"Then let's start with an episode from early in Jesus' ministry that is recorded in Matthew (Mt 9:1-8), Mark (Mk 2:1-12), and Luke (Lk 5:17-26). It takes place in a house where Jesus is preaching. The house is so crowded that no one else can possibly get in. Enter a group of men carrying a paralytic on a mat. They are eager to get their friend to Jesus in hopes that Jesus will heal him, but the crowd will not let them pass. Desperate to help their friend, they finally climb on the roof and lower the man through it."

"That must have gotten the homeowner upset!"

"I'm sure it did, but whether they were right or wrong to do it, it did bring the paralyzed man in direct contact with Jesus. Impressed by the faith of the paralytic's friends, Jesus looks at the sick man and says, 'Your sins are forgiven.'

"This upsets the Pharisees and the teachers of the law very much. They begin to mutter under their breath that Jesus is speaking blasphemy, for only God can forgive sins. But Jesus hears their grumbles and tells them that he, as the Son of Man, has the authority to forgive sins on the earth. Then he heals the paralytic and tells him to take up his mat and go home.

"Now, Reza, I would like to clarify what is going on in this story by means of an illustration. What would you think if I walked over to you and punched you on the nose; and then, while you were holding your nose to stop the blood from running on to your shirt, David walked over to me and said, 'That's OK, I forgive you'?"

"That would be ridiculous."

"Why would it be ridiculous?"

"Because David can't forgive you."

"Why not?"

"Because he's not the person you hurt. Only the person you hurt can forgive you for hurting him."

"Ah, so you are saying that only you, Reza, can forgive me for punching you on the nose."

"Yes."

"Now, when we commit a sin, the person we are ultimately hurting is God. True, we may sometimes hurt another person through our sin, but the offended party when we commit a sin that breaks God's law is finally God himself. Do you agree?"

"Yes."

"Under normal circumstances, Jesus telling the paralytic that his sins are forgiven is as ridiculous as David forgiving me for punching you on the nose. But in Jesus' case, it is more than ridiculous; it is blasphemous. For Jesus, by claiming the power to forgive the paralytic's sins, is claiming to be equal with God. That's why the Pharisees get mad and accuse him of blasphemy. In fact, if Jesus were not equal with God, then the Pharisees would have been *right* to call him a blasphemer."

"But why does Jesus call himself the Son of Man rather than the Son of God?"

"That's a good question," I said as I walked over to the bookshelf and took down a Bible. "In the Old Testament, the phrase 'Son of Man' was a messianic title: that is to say, one of the titles the promised Messiah would bear. It is used in an amazing passage in the book of Daniel. In a vision in the night, the prophet Daniel sees the following:

> Behold, with the clouds of heaven
> there came one like a son of man,
> and he came to the Ancient of Days
> and was presented before him.
> And to him was given dominion
> and glory and a kingdom,
> that all peoples, nations, and languages
> should serve him;
> his dominion is an everlasting dominion,
> which shall not pass away,
> and his kingdom one
> that shall not be destroyed. (Dan 7:13-14)

"The Ancient of Days is God himself, but the one Daniel calls the Son of Man is clearly equal with the Ancient of Days and will be given all power and authority. After Daniel made that prophecy, no one in the Bible but Jesus took the title for himself."

"But how do we know that Jesus had that passage in mind?"

"When Jesus was put on trial by the high priest Caiaphas, he was asked, point blank, 'I adjure you by the living God, tell us if you are the Christ [the Greek word for "Messiah"], the Son of God.' In response, Jesus says, 'You have said so,' but he then continues to say, 'But I tell you, from now on you will see the Son of Man seated at the right hand of Power and coming on the clouds of heaven' (Mt 26:63-64). In response, Caiaphas tears his clothes and accuses Jesus of blasphemy (Mt 25:65).

"This passage tells us two important things: first, that Jesus claimed to be both the Son of God and Son of Man and that he identified himself with the messianic prophecy from Daniel; second, that the high priest of the Jews recognized Jesus' claims as being blasphemous. In fact, Jesus was condemned by the Jewish Council, or Sanhedrin, precisely because he claimed to be the Son of God. He was not condemned for being a prophet but for claiming to be equal with God."

"Are there other examples where Jesus makes claims like this during his ministry and the Jewish leaders accuse him of blasphemy?"

"There is a very powerful example in the Gospel of John where Jesus and the Pharisees are debating Jesus' relationship to Abraham. As you know, Reza, Jews, Christians, and Muslims all look to Abraham as their spiritual father."

"That is true. Abraham is a great prophet in the Qur'an who worshiped the one true God and fought against the idolatry of his times."

"He was a great prophet indeed! In the dialogue John records, Jesus angers the Pharisees by telling them they are not true sons of Abraham. If they were, they would not be seeking to kill Jesus (Jn 8:39-40).

"As the dialogue gets more heated, Jesus makes a startling proclamation, one that exceeds anything a prophet would dare to say: 'Truly, truly, I say to you, if anyone keeps my word, he will never see death' (Jn 8:51). To this bold claim the Pharisees react: 'Now we know that you have a demon! Abraham died, as did the prophets, yet you say, "If anyone keeps my word, he will never taste death." Are you greater than our father Abraham, who died? And the prophets died! Who do you make yourself out to be?' (Jn 8:52-53).

"Do you see, Reza? The Pharisees are well aware that no true prophet would make so audacious a claim. Prophets proclaim the words God gave them, but they do not claim power over life and death. Jesus here claims to be something more than a prophet. Would you like to know what happens next?"

"I would."

"Jesus responds that his glory comes from God and that it is he, not the Pharisees, who knows God. Then he concludes with a verse that would be the height of arrogance and presumption if Jesus were not far more than a prophet: 'Your father Abraham rejoiced that he would see my day. He saw it and was glad' (Jn 8:56).

"Now listen to how the dialogue ends: 'So the Jews said to him, "You are not yet fifty years old, and have you seen Abraham?" Jesus said to them, "Truly, truly, I say to you, before Abraham was, I am." So they picked up stones to throw at him, but Jesus hid himself and went out of the temple' (Jn 8:57-59)."

"Why do the Pharisees try to stone him?"

"Because Jesus, if he is only a prophet, has just spoken unutterable blasphemy. And he has done so in two ways. First of all, by saying that he existed before Abraham, he claims to partake somehow in the eternal nature of God. But the blasphemy goes much deeper than that. Notice that Jesus does not say, 'before Abraham was, I was,' but 'before Abraham was, I am.' That may not strike us as a statement worthy of stoning, but it was to the Pharisees."

"Why?"

"Because 'I am' was the divine name God revealed to Moses when he spoke to him from the burning bush."

"Yes, the story of the burning bush is also in the Qur'an (20:9-14; 27:7-9), but please explain to me about this 'I am.'"

"In Exodus, the second book of the Torah, Moses asks God his name, and God responds that his name is 'I AM WHO I AM' (Ex 3:13-14). That is to say, God is the one being who has always existed: He had no beginning and will have no end. That name, 'I AM WHO I AM,' comes from the Hebrew verb 'to be,' and is written as *Jehovah* or *Yahweh*. However, that name was so holy that the Jews never spoke it. In the Old Testament the name is written as LORD. When Jesus identifies himself with the 'I AM,' the Pharisees know what he is claiming, and that is why they immediately try to stone him, which was the prescribed method for killing blasphemers (Lev 24:16)."

"I must admit that these are very strong arguments. Are there other places where Jesus links himself to the 'I AM?'"

"Actually, throughout the Gospel of John, Jesus makes startling 'I am' claims. Here is a list of them: 'I am the bread of life' (Jn 6:35), 'I am the light of the world' (Jn 8:12), 'I am the door' (Jn 10:9), 'I am the good shepherd' (Jn 10:11), 'I am the resurrection and the life' (Jn 11:25), 'I am the way, the truth, and the life' (Jn 14:6), and 'I am the true vine' (Jn 15:1). I must say that I am particularly fond of 'I am the way, the truth, and the life,' for that is the founding verse of my university!"

Reza was about to respond when a voice shouted out from the kitchen: "Dad, why don't you mention C. S. Lewis's liar-lunatic-Lord argument?"

The voice belonged to my son, who must have snuck in from the back door.

My son, Alex, who is twenty-one months older than his sister, had just arrived from San Antonio. At least in his case, it turned out to be a good thing that the turkey had not yet arrived!

Alex was now in his second year teaching third through fifth grade Latin at Geneva, a classical Christian school located in the idyllic town of Boerne. He had majored in history and classics and was enjoying opening young minds and hearts to the wonders and beauties of the Latin language.

Alex was a big fan of audiobooks, and he had already listened to a few dozen books as he commuted back and forth between San Antonio and Boerne. As it so happened, during his traffic-impeded five-hour drive from San Antonio, he had been listening to the audiobook of Lewis's *Mere Christianity*. That is why, when he quietly entered the house and heard his father discussing an issue famously covered by Lewis in book two, chapter three of *Mere Christianity*, he could not help but shout out his suggestion.

"Welcome home, Alex," I cried, leaping from my chair and crossing the room to give him a hug. "I'm so glad you made it before dinner."

I'm not sure the hungry guests in the den shared my gladness, but they were nice enough not to say so. Stacey, meanwhile, gave her brother a hug as well and invited him to sit next to her on the couch.

"Alex," I said, "this is Reza, and we are discussing whether Jesus actually claimed to be the Son of God. I explained to him that not just Muslims but many who call themselves Christians believe that Jesus was not the Son of God but only a prophet."

"But that is not a tenable position to take," said Alex, "as C. S. Lewis proves logically in his liar-lunatic-Lord argument."

"Alex, your arrival couldn't have been better timed. I just finished demonstrating from the Gospels that Jesus made claims to be equal with God: that is, to have the power to forgive sins, to be both the Son of Man and the Son of God, and to share in the eternal, 'I Am' nature of God. If you would, please take over from here and explain why Lewis argues that, given Jesus' claims, it is not tenable to say he was only a prophet."

"Well," said Alex, "a man who made the claims that Jesus made but who was not the Son of God would not be a prophet. He might be crazy—there are plenty of people in insane asylums who think they are God or Jesus—or a terrible deceiver, but he could not be a prophet. In fact, if Jesus was not the Son of God, then the Pharisees were right to condemn him for blasphemy and turn him over to the Romans to be crucified. Jesus simply did not leave us with the option of calling him a good man and a prophet but nothing more. If he was not the Lord, then he was either a lunatic or a liar."

"Well said, Alex. I believe that the logic of Lewis's argument is airtight. If you read the Gospels carefully, by the way, you will find that Jesus' enemies invariably accused him of being either a blasphemer or demon possessed (Mk 3:22). At the start of his ministry, Jesus' own family thought he was crazy (Mk 3:21). Those who opposed Jesus never said he was just a teacher. They recognized the enormity of his claims but refused to acknowledge and worship him as the Son of God. That left them with no other option but to attack him as a liar or a lunatic."

"That is a strong argument," said Reza, "but, if I may, can't the same liar-lunatic-lord argument be used for Muhammad?"

"I don't believe it can, Reza," I replied. "Like all the holy men and prophets of history from Abraham to Moses, Buddha to Confucius, Socrates to the Persian Zoroaster, Muhammad only claimed to have heard a word from God. He might have heard that word clearly or vaguely, but his claim to have heard does not make him a liar, lunatic, or lord.

"I would venture to guess that everyone in this room has felt, at some time in his life, that he has heard a word from God. We might be partly right or partly wrong about what we heard. Perhaps we did hear it clearly, but the word was only meant for us and not for everyone else. In any case, we are not therefore liars, lunatics, or lords.

"But Jesus, in sharp contrast, did not merely claim to hear from God. He claimed to be one with God. Prophets such as Muhammad say to their followers, 'I will show you the way; I will teach you the truth; I will guide you to a fuller life.' But that is not what Jesus said. He said, 'I *am* the way; I *am* the truth; I *am* the life.' Jesus made claims about himself and not just about his message.

"Let's say I were to stand up now, deliver a complicated forty-five-minute lecture on Christian theology, and then leave the house to see whether I could find our missing turkey." (I got a few laughs when I said that!) "Then, five minutes after I left, my son, Alex, here stood up and interpreted my lecture. Well, his interpretation might be completely correct or partly correct or mostly wrong. But you wouldn't categorize him as either a liar or a lunatic or a lord.

"But, let's say that instead of merely interpreting my lecture, he stood up and announced to you all that he *was* Louis Markos! Well, either he would be trying to deceive you, or he would be crazy, or he would in fact be Louis Markos.

"In the Qur'an, Muhammad claims only to be the mouthpiece of God. That is why the entire Qur'an is written in the first person. It is not Muhammad who speaks but God who speaks through him. Isn't that correct, Reza?"

"It is. The word *Qur'an* means 'recitation' in Arabic, for we believe that it was dictated to Muhammad by the archangel Gabriel."

"Since Jesus was also a prophet, there are times when he simply passes on the word of God to the Jews. But he goes further than that. Again and again, he says things like the following: 'For whoever is ashamed of me and of my words in this adulterous and sinful generation, of him will the Son of Man also be ashamed when he comes in the glory of his Father with the holy angels' (Mk 8:38).

"Do you hear that? We must not just accept the message; we must not be ashamed of the messenger. Jesus puts the focus on himself in a way that no good prophet would do. More than that, he says that if we are ashamed of *him*, *he* will be ashamed of us, and that will have terrible consequences when he comes in glory with his Father. A man who was merely a prophet would not speak of himself coming in glory."

"I'm sorry to jump in here," said a young female voice behind me, "but I would like to ask a question of my own."

The voice belonged to one of my undergraduate students whose parents had immigrated to America from India. Her name was Sita (SEE-tah), and she was a nursing major. Sita had grown up in a Hindu home but had expressed interest before in Christianity, especially in the person of Christ, whom she felt drawn to as a figure of love and acceptance.

"Please do ask your question, Sita," I said.

"I'd like to, but I'm afraid I might offend you."

"I am never offended by sincere questions. Jesus certainly wasn't!"

"Well, I've listened to what you've been saying about Jesus' claims, and it seems to me that there would be no liar-lunatic-lord dilemma if Jesus were a Hindu."

"Sita, this might surprise you, but I agree with you!"

"You do?"

"Yes. If you were to ask a Muslim or Jew whether Jesus was the Son of God, he would answer, 'God has no son.' But if you were to ask a Hindu or Buddhist whether Jesus was the Son of God, he would probably say yes but then add, 'So were Buddha and Confucius and Gandhi . . . and all of us, if we only knew it.'"

"Yes, that is what I mean. Why can't we say that Jesus was the Son of God in the way that we all are?"

"The reason we can't say that is that Jesus was a Jew, a radical monotheist who worshiped a transcendent God who created the universe and dwells apart from it. In Hinduism and Buddhism, on the other hand, God is immanent—that is to say, he pervades all of nature and is in fact one with it.

"Sita, do you remember the scene in the *Gita* when Krishna reveals himself to the warrior Arjuna?"

"I do. That is one of my favorite parts. Arjuna asks Krishna, who is an avatar of Vishnu, to show himself to him. Krishna does, and Arjuna realizes that Krishna is everything: He is the grass and the trees and the water and the sky. He is all thought, all life, all intelligence. And he is all the gods as well."

"Yes, in the end, it turns out that the countless gods of Hinduism are but the many faces of Krishna. Sita, do you remember the central, three-word message of the *Gita*?"

"Brahman is atman."

"I'm proud of you, Sita! You really know your stuff!

"In Hinduism," she continued, smiling at my compliment, "Brahman is the all, the impersonal force that has no beginning and no ending and that extends through all things. Atman, in contrast, is the individual soul. When one reaches the highest level of enlightenment in Hinduism, one realizes that there is no final distinction between Brahman and our own atman. All is one."

"Excellent!" I exclaimed. "What you just described so well is what philosophers of religion call monism. If Jesus had been a monist, then Sita's point would be true. Jesus would just be saying what many enlightened Buddhas have said before: that he is one with the universe just as we all would be if we could only tear away the veil that keeps us in ignorance of the true nature of reality."

"But doesn't Jesus say a prayer in which he asks God to make all of his disciples one just as he and the Father are one?"

"Wow, Sita, you really *have* been studying these issues. I'm impressed! The prayer you mention is part of John 13–17, also known as the Upper

Room Discourse. These beautiful chapters record Jesus' last night with his disciples. Instead of describing the Last Supper, as Matthew, Mark, and Luke had already done, John the disciple, who was an eyewitness of that final night, records all the intimate things Jesus shared with his disciples after Judas left to betray him.

"During the Upper Room Discourse, Jesus commissions his disciples with a difficult task. After he is crucified, it will be up to them to carry on his message. That is why Jesus begins his long discourse by giving them a new commandment that will allow the world to recognize them as Jesus' true disciples and witnesses on earth: 'A new commandment I give to you, that you love one another: just as I have loved you, you also are to love one another. By this all people will know that you are my disciples, if you have love for one another' (Jn 13:34-35)."

"Yes," said Sita with a smile, "I love that verse."

"If only all Christians lived up to it, a lot more people would be drawn to Christ. Jesus calls his followers to unity, but it is a unity of love. We continue to be separate individuals, but we are now controlled by love rather than competition and the survival of the fittest. We also, by loving others, point to a higher unity, but that is the unity not of monism but of the Trinity—that the one God is his own community, for he exists eternally as Father, Son, and Holy Spirit."

"That still sounds a bit monistic."

"If we jump ahead a few verses, we find Jesus offering this startling answer to Philip the disciple's request that Jesus show them the Father: 'Have I been with you so long, and you still do not know me, Philip? Whoever has seen me has seen the Father. How can you say, "Show us the Father"? Do you not believe that I am in the Father and the Father is in me?' (Jn 14:9-10).

"If Jesus were a true monist, Sita, he would not tell Philip that he must look on him to see the Father; he would teach him the 'higher' truth that if he truly looks at himself, he will see God. But Jesus does not teach that Brahman is atman. Rather, he teaches that God is revealed fully only in Jesus.

"Directly in between the two verses I just quoted, Jesus makes that startling claim I mentioned earlier, 'I am the way, the truth, and the life,' after which he adds, 'No one comes to the Father except through me' (Jn 14:6). If

Jesus were a monist, he would not say he was the only way to the Father. Any guru or teacher who had achieved enlightenment and discovered that Brahman is atman could conduct us to God. But that is not what Jesus says. He claims to be the one-and-only mediator between God and man.

"The amazing message of the Gospels, but especially of the Upper Room Discourse, is that only by being in Christ can we be in God. That is to say, if we are in Christ and Christ is in God, then through him we will be in God. And if we do that, then we will share in the love and unity of the Trinity. That is why Jesus prays at the close of the Upper Room Discourse those beautiful words you alluded to earlier: 'I in them and you in me, that they may become perfectly one, so that the world may know that you sent me and loved them even as you loved me' (Jn 17:23). It is through our unity in love that we will reveal to the world the love of God and the truth of Christ."

"I have often caught glimpses of that love at Houston Christian. It is that love, in fact, that has made me want to learn more about Jesus."

"I'm glad to hear that, Sita. That is one of the reasons I have continued to teach at HCU for over twenty-five years!

"But let me conclude by pointing to one more aspect of the Upper Room Discourse that helps make clear why Jesus' call to unity is not a call to monism. All of John 17 is devoted to Jesus' prayer for his disciples. At the beginning of that prayer, he says: 'And now, Father, glorify me in your own presence with the glory that I had with you before the world existed' (Jn 17:5). This claim, that Jesus shared in the Father's glory before the world was made, is a claim that he never extends to his disciples, or to any other human being, for that matter. We, like the angels, are created beings; only Jesus shares in the uncreated nature of the Trinity.

"Indeed, even when we are unified with God and Jesus in heaven, we will still, Jesus claims at the end of his prayer, look upon his glory: 'Father, I desire that they also, whom you have given me, may be with me where I am, to see my glory that you have given me because you loved me before the foundation of the world' (Jn 17:24). If our destiny is to all be one, then there would be no separate us to look upon his glory."

"But, but," said Reza, whom I could see was getting a bit restless, "there is one more problem with all of the things you've been saying."

"What's that, Reza?"

"All your arguments are based on quotes from the Bible. How do we know that Jesus actually said the things recorded in the Gospels? Couldn't they have been corrupted or changed by later Christians to back up their teachings?"

I closed my eyes and silently counted to five. Then I opened them. Still no turkey!

3

ARE THE GOSPELS HISTORICAL?

"REZA," I SAID, "I HAVE READ SOME PAMPHLETS written by Muslim apologists in which they claim that we cannot trust the Gospels as we now have them because they have been corrupted. Have you also read pamphlets like that?"

"I have," he said, "and I've found some of them convincing. We don't have the original manuscripts, so how can we know the Gospels we have today are authentic?"

"Reza, there are many scholars who were raised in Christian homes who have made these claims. In a little bit I will explain the problem with their arguments. But first I want to emphasize that although skeptical Christians might be able to make that argument, believing Muslims really cannot."

"Why not? That is a strange point to make."

"The reason I make it, Reza, is that we possess full copies of the New Testament that date back to the middle of the fourth century AD. That is to say, we have complete copies, not just of the Gospels but of the whole New Testament, that are two centuries older than Muhammad and the Qur'an."

"Why is that important?"

"Because it means that, even if it could be shown that our manuscripts are different from the ones originally written in the first century, the Bible Muhammad had available to him is the same one we have today. And that is important because Muhammad, as we discussed earlier, considered the Gospels to be divinely revealed."

"I must admit that that is a good argument. But I am still interested to know why you think we can trust the accuracy of the Gospels when we don't have the original manuscripts."

"Reza, let me begin by doing something that I always enjoy doing: putting my lovely daughter on the spot. Stacey," I said, turning to face her, "can you please list for us some of the Greek and Roman books you read during your first year in the honors college?"

"Sure," she said, without batting an eye. "We read Homer's two epics, the *Iliad* and *Odyssey*; a number of Greek tragedies, including Aeschylus's *Oresteia* and the *Oedipus* and *Antigone* of Sophocles; the histories of Herodotus and Thucydides; seven or eight dialogues of Plato; the *Nicomachean Ethics* of Aristotle; Virgil's *Aeneid*; Ovid's *Metamorphoses*; a number of speeches by Cicero and poems by Horace; and some of the historical writings of Livy and Plutarch. Shall I go on?"

"I think you've listed enough," I said and turned to face everyone else and share my pride that my daughter had read all those books in just her first year in the HCU honors college.

"Now, Reza, if you were to visit universities across the country—not private Christian ones like HCU but public secular ones—and ask the various professors whether they felt they could trust the manuscripts we have today of Homer, Aeschylus, Sophocles, Herodotus, Thucydides, Plato, Aristotle, Virgil, Ovid, Cicero, Horace, Livy, and Plutarch, you would find an overwhelming consensus that we can trust that the works we have today are quite close to the ones those authors wrote so many centuries ago. Of course, there will be scribal errors here and there, as there are even with many of the plays of Shakespeare, but that does not mean we cannot trust their essential accuracy."

"Of course," said Reza. "I don't think anyone would dispute that."

"But we don't have original manuscripts for any of the works that Stacey listed. What we have are just a few handwritten copies from well over five hundred years later. Alex, do you remember reading Julius Caesar's *Gallic Wars* in Latin class?"

"I do. I really enjoyed translating Caesar's wonderfully clear Latin!"

"You may be surprised to know that the oldest copy we have of the *Gallic Wars* dates from eight hundred years after Caesar, and we have very few copies at that. And yet, no one argues that the text we have today for *Gallic Wars* is radically untrustworthy. Our oldest copies of the histories of Herodotus and Thucydides date to after AD 800, a full thirteen hundred years after they were written. And we only have about ten handwritten copies of each.

"And the same goes for all the works Stacey read, works that serve as the foundation for Western culture. The only books she listed that boast more than one hundred handwritten copies are Homer's two epics. But does anyone want to guess the time lag between Homer and the earliest of those copies?"

"Five hundred years," said Stacey.

"No, seven hundred," said Alex.

"Actually, it's about one thousand years. And yet, there is no book outside the Bible that is more foundational to Western civilization.

"OK, if that is the case for Homer, how many handwritten copies do you think we have of the New Testament in Greek?"

"Five hundred?"

"A thousand?"

"Try five thousand," I said with a smile. "As I said a moment ago, the oldest complete one comes 250 to 300 years later, but we have significant portions of the Gospels and the letters of Paul that date as early as AD 200, and we have a scrap of the Gospel of John that dates to about AD 110. And those are just the ones in Greek. We have thousands more manuscripts if you count copies in other ancient languages."

"That's impressive," said Reza.

"It is, and it highlights the simple fact that if we cannot trust that the New Testament we have is an accurate reflection of the original manuscripts, then we cannot trust any of the books from antiquity. Heck, we can't trust most of the works from the Middle Ages either. To put it simply, if the New Testament weren't the New Testament, no scholar would be attacking its authenticity and reliability. It's only because the Bible is now judged by its critics by radically different criteria than they would use for any other pre-printing press book that they can claim the Gospels are unreliable."

"But I have read," said Reza, "that all those copies of the New Testament that you mention are riddled with variations and inconsistencies."

"Luckily, Reza, a book came out back in 2014 by a highly respected biblical textual scholar named Craig Blomberg that puts many of those rumors to rest. Bart Ehrman, who was raised in a Christian home but later rejected the faith because he came to reject the authority of the New Testament, often attacks the historical reliability of the Gospels. In a book he wrote titled *Misquoting Jesus*, he touts the fact that there are four hundred thousand textual variants among our manuscripts of the New Testament."

"That sounds like pretty damning evidence to me."

"It does until you put it in context, as Bloomberg does in his book *Can We Still Believe the Bible?* I actually memorized what he said because it is so impressive. When you take Ehrman's huge number and spread it out across the many thousands of manuscripts, it comes out to sixteen variants per manuscript. But those variants are so unbelievably minor that only one-tenth of 1 percent are listed in the footnotes of Bibles printed today.

"I would encourage you all," I said, looking around the room, "to get a modern translation of the Bible that includes footnotes that catalog those variants. You will find that none of them affects any major teaching or doctrine of the church. Even the ethical teachings of Jesus are not affected by these variations. And even when you find a single verse that might be a little bit unclear, you will find other verses in the Bible where that bit of non-clarity is rendered perfectly clear.

"Really," I added, "there are only two variations that are substantial, but even they don't change anything."

"What are they?" asked Reza.

"The last portion of Mark (Mk 16:9-20) that lists several of Jesus' resurrection appearances is questioned. It seems to have been added on later. On its own, that *would* pose a problem, since the resurrection is the central miraculous claim of the whole Bible, but the material listed in that contested passage appears clearly in Matthew, Luke, and John. And the uncontested part of the last chapter of Mark does attest to the fact that the tomb of Jesus was empty when Mary Magdalene appeared to anoint the body."

"What is the other one?"

"I'm sure many of you know the famous story in John 8 when a woman caught in adultery is brought before Jesus. When the crowd asks Jesus whether they should stone her, Jesus says that he among them who is without sin should cast the first stone."

"I like that story," said Sita.

"So do I! But no one is sure whether it originally belonged at that place in John's Gospel. It could have appeared elsewhere, or maybe was added later."

"I hope the story is true," said Sita. "It sounds so true to Jesus' character."

"I'm glad you said that, Sita. Although it is possible that it was added later, I would submit that everyone who reads the Gospels recognizes the truth of that story. What I mean is that we all have a strong sense that it is something that Jesus *would* say."

"I don't get your point," said Reza.

"What I'm trying to say is that there is no more real figure from the ancient world. Yes, we get to know people like Pericles of Greece and Xerxes of Persia, Hannibal of Carthage and Caesar Augustus of Rome. But none of them has the full, rounded reality of Jesus. If I were to read you a list of actions and sayings and ask you if they sounded like the kinds of things Jesus would do or say, I bet you would agree in your answers. Only Socrates comes anywhere near Jesus in his stubborn, flesh-and-blood personhood. No one could have made up Jesus. He is too real, too tangible."

"But what about the Gnostic Gospels?" said a voice from the hallway.

The voice belonged to an American named Bill in his early forties who had been talking on his cellphone in the dining room. His ears had perked up when he heard us speaking in the den about the authority of the New Testament, and he had moved into the hallway to listen.

Bill had become a believer in Christ some seven years earlier, but his faith had been challenged by writers such as Bart Ehrman who questioned the validity and reliability of the Gospels. He was a sincere man and a highly logical thinker who had little patience for blind faith. He knew that faith meant believing in things that you cannot see, but he nevertheless expected that faith to be reasonable and based on trustworthy evidence.

"Bill," I said, "you raise an important issue. There are indeed a number of other Gospels about Jesus, but they are all much later, with the earliest in the middle of the second century and the others later than that. By the time the Gnostic Gospels appeared, everyone who had known or heard Jesus or one of his disciples had been long dead. The canonical Gospels, on the other hand, were written by eyewitnesses and at a time when their testimony, if it were false, could have been contradicted by other eyewitnesses."

"How do you mean?"

"Matthew and John were both disciples of Jesus and so knew him personally. Mark did not know Jesus, but he was an early Christian who became the right-hand man of the apostle Peter. In fact, many Bible scholars like to refer to the Gospel of Mark as the Gospel of Peter. Luke was also not a disciple, but he worked alongside Paul, and he spent many years interviewing eyewitnesses. It is clear from reading the opening chapters of his Gospel that he even interviewed the Virgin Mary herself."

"But the Gospels were written thirty or even forty years after Jesus died. Doesn't that make them suspect?"

"Imagine if I were to write a history about the Vietnam War and were to make claims that were blatantly wrong about that war, how it was fought, and who its key players were. Even though the Vietnam War took place forty years ago, there are still plenty of veterans and government officials from that time alive to stand up and proclaim that my book was false."

"But what if they accepted your facts but disputed your interpretation of them?"

"Good point. That is exactly what the enemies of Christianity said. They continued to maintain that Jesus was a blasphemer worthy of death. But none of them attacked the Gospels by saying that Jesus never did or said what the Gospels record him as saying. Heck, those who opposed Jesus and

Christianity did not even deny that Christ performed miracles; rather, they claimed that he did so by the power of the devil."

"All right, but let's get back to the Gnostic Gospels. Why shouldn't they be taken as seriously as Matthew, Mark, Luke, and John?"

"First of all, the Gnostic Gospels presuppose the existence of the four canonical Gospels. In many ways, they exist parasitically on them. Second, the Gnostic Gospels, unlike the canonical ones, are radically unhistorical."

"Why do you say that?"

"Let's play a thought game. Read one of the Gnostic Gospels, say, the Gospel of Thomas or the Gospel of Philip. Then read it again, but this time replace Jesus with Buddha. You will find that the change makes no difference whatsoever to the message of Thomas or Philip. The Gnostic Gospels do not present a real, historical Jesus living in a real, historical Palestine, as do the canonical Gospels. They simply string together esoteric sayings without any kind of real historical context, hoping that the claim that Jesus said them will give them some kind of legitimacy."

"But can't the same thing be said about the Gospels in the New Testament?"

"No. The canonical Gospels are remarkably true to history. I'm sure you have heard about the Dead Sea Scrolls."

"I have, but I'm surprised you mention them, as I have heard that they take away from the authority of the New Testament."

"I've heard those rumors as well, but they are not true. Far from contradicting anything in the New Testament, the Dead Sea Scrolls add indirectly to their authenticity."

"What do you mean by 'indirectly'?"

"Well, they can't offer direct evidence for the New Testament since they were written in the century before Christ. But they provide indirect evidence by offering a picture of Palestine that fits with what we read in the New Testament. The canonical Gospels are not, like the Gnostic Gospels, set in a timeless world of meditation but in a historically accurate world that includes Pharisees and Sadducees, synagogues and the Sanhedrin, and that is acted out against real artifacts, geography, and political forces.

"But even you must admit that there are lots of contradictions in the Gospels."

"It depends on what you mean by *contradictions*. If you mean slight discrepancies in the details of stories and the perspective from which they are told, then there are quite a number in the Gospels and plenty more in the Bible as a whole. But if you mean actual contradictions of fact that offer an inconsistent picture of history or philosophy or theology, then they do not."

"What's the difference?"

"Too often today, people hold up the Bible to a verification system that did not exist when it was written, that in fact has only existed since the Enlightenment. The Bible never claims to be a scientific textbook, or for that matter a textbook at all. If the Bible were trying to fit itself to a modern notion of truth, then there would be only one Gospel, not four. The Bible is not concerned with the kind of mathematical, logical positivist kind of accuracy we look for in an experimental lab.

"Don't get me wrong. The Gospel of Luke is a carefully researched and written historical book of the life of Christ that dates itself in accordance with the key political figures of the day and that presents a reliable, highly accurate picture of Jesus' world that can be verified by historians and archaeologists. But its goal is to present eyewitness evidence shaped into a narrative, not to hold up a camera and let it record things."

"Then why do parallel accounts in Matthew, Mark, and Luke of the same episode contain different details?"

"For the same reason that if you listen to three different eyewitness accounts of a crime during a trial, they will differ slightly. I am thinking here of three honest, accurate, reliable eyewitness accounts, not ones that are false. Actually, if all three accounts were exactly the same, then an honest judge would be rightly skeptical."

"That's a fair point."

"But there is another reason, based on some excellent recent research, to accept those discrepant details in the Gospels as a narrative technique that does not rob the Gospels of their accuracy."

"I'd be interested to hear it."

"As one of my colleagues, Mike Licona, has shown, the secular biographies of Plutarch, which were written in the same century as the Gospels, use the same historical technique as the Gospels. Plutarch wrote several biographies that overlap and thus reference the same episode. This happens, for example, in his biographies of Julius Caesar, Brutus, and Marc Antony. Although Plutarch wrote all three of those biographies himself, and though he knew that the same readers would read them, when he tells the same story in different biographies, he changes both details and perspective."

"Why does he do that?"

"For the same reason the Gospel writers do, to offer a perspective that fits with the focus of their biography. They are not changing the evidence, merely arranging it in a way that will fit together and make sense. That is how the best and most reliable histories are told: not as a chronological but disjointed stream of undigested facts, figures, and dates but as a continuous narrative that unites those details."

"I see your point. But that does not prove the Gospels were divinely inspired."

"Bill, as a Christian, I do indeed believe that the Bible was directly inspired by God, but you must understand that the arguments I have been making today do not rely on a belief that the Gospels were God-breathed. As long as we can trust the Gospels to provide a reliable record of the deeds and words of Jesus, and I hope I have offered some good evidence for that, then the liar-lunatic-Lord argument Alex summarized for us maintains its logical force."

"Yes, I am familiar with that argument, and I am certainly not willing to argue that Jesus was a liar or a lunatic. But isn't it true that the idea that Jesus was fully man and fully God was put together at the Council of Nicaea in 325?"

"Oh my," I said with slight weariness in my voice, "You're referring to *The Da Vinci Code*, aren't you?"

"Yes."

When most people think of *The Da Vinci Code* by Dan Brown, they immediately think of his finally ludicrous claim that Jesus married Mary Magdalene and had children with her. As that claim is too silly to take seriously,

I tend to ignore it, but Brown makes another, subtler charge in his entertaining, fast-paced novel that, if it were true, would call in to doubt the very foundations of Christianity.

"Bill," I said after gathering my thoughts, "I take it that what you have in mind is Brown's argument that Christian theology was essentially made up when Constantine, after ending the Roman persecution of the church, called all the bishops to meet in modern-day Turkey for the Council of Nicaea. It was there, of course, that they hammered out the Nicene Creed on which basic Christian doctrine rests."

"That is exactly what I have in mind."

"Bill, I believe that you work in a big office."

"I do."

"Imagine it is, say, the 1980s, and another office not far from yours goes through a terrible sexual harassment lawsuit that causes the office to close. After that happened, what do you think your office would have done?"

"The office managers would have gotten together, written up a sexual harassment policy, and had all of us sign it."

"Exactly. But when they made up that policy, would they have made it up out of thin air, or would they have based it on unspoken expectations of proper male-female behavior that were always understood but had never been written in stone before?"

"The latter, certainly. The understanding would have been there, but it would not have been written up as official policy until the threat from the neighboring office made it necessary to do so."

"What you describe, Bill, is precisely the situation in the fourth century when Constantine called for the Council of Nicaea. Christians knew and understood the foundations of their faith—in particular, the incarnation, with its belief that Jesus was the unique God-man—but they did not have to put it in official philosophical language until Christian orthodoxy was threatened from within."

"What threat do you mean?"

"The threat of Arianism. Arius was a heretical church leader who had been proclaiming that Jesus was not divine but a lesser being. His claim contradicted what the Christian church had been teaching for 250 years.

Indeed, if the church had not been preaching the incarnation for well over two centuries, then the teachings of Arius would not have been considered so controversial and disruptive. It was the threat of Arius's teachings that made the council necessary."

"But what proof do we have that the Christians had been preaching what we today call Christianity for over two centuries?"

"As it so happens, we do have proof of that, proof that even secular critics of Christianity do not dispute. In addition to the New Testament, we have several other early church documents that come a generation or two after the Gospels and offer commentary on them. The two earliest of these are the Epistle of Clement, what we call 1 Clement, fourth bishop of Rome, and the seven epistles of Ignatius, third bishop of Antioch."

"When were they written?"

"That is the amazing part. The critical consensus of Christian and secular scholars alike is that Clement's letter was written about 96 and Ignatius's letters about 110. That means they give us direct insight into the beliefs of the first two generations of Christians. If you read them, you will find that the basic doctrines of Christianity are already there in their full. Those doctrines did not come later but were there from the beginning."

"You will need to elaborate."

"If you read Clement, you will find that he expresses a full and nuanced understanding of the divinity of Christ and of how he won our salvation through the shedding of his blood on the cross. In addition, throughout his epistle, he treats both the Old and New Testaments as being fully inspired by the Holy Spirit and canonical. Indeed, he backs up all he says with quotes from the Bible. The fact that he does so offers strong evidence that the New Testament, together with the Old, was already in circulation.

"Clement explains, with wonderful clarity, how the life, death, and resurrection of Jesus fulfilled the prophecies of the Old Testament; he even quotes many of them, emphasizing the same ones that Christians most often quote today: in particular, Psalm 22, which reads like an eyewitness account of the crucifixion, even though it was written hundreds of years before crucifixion existed; and Isaiah 53, which explains, seven hundred years before Jesus, how the Messiah would take upon himself the sins of the world."

"Does he use the word *Trinity*?"

"Good point! He does not use it, just as the New Testament does not use it, for that word came later. It was coined by later philosophers and theologians to provide a name for the unique relationship between the Father, Son, and Holy Spirit. But the name did not create the relationship. The relationship came first and was given a name later when the writings of heretics such as Arius made it necessary to do so.

"Jesus himself laid out that relationship clearly when he commissioned his disciples, shortly before his ascension into heaven, to 'make disciples of all nations, baptizing them in the name of the Father and of the Son and of the Holy Spirit' (Mt 28:19). Note that he uses the singular word *name* to refer to all three. Paul also uses trinitarian language, treating Father, Son, and Holy Spirit as one (2 Cor 13:14)."

"What about Clement?"

"Stacey, can you—?"

"I'm way ahead of you, Dad," said Stacey, handing me my copy of *Early Christian Writings*. She had read the book herself in the honors college, so she knew right where to find it in my office.

"Thank you, my dear," I said. "You are a most excellent daughter!'"

As Stacey smiled, I turned to chapter 58 of Clement's epistle and read aloud this great promise:

> As surely as God lives, as Jesus Christ lives, and the Holy Ghost also (on whom are set the faith and hope of God's elect), so surely the man who keeps the divinely appointed decrees and statutes with humility and an unfailing consideration for others, and never looks back, will be enrolled in honour among the number of those who are saved through Jesus Christ, by whom is God glorified for ever and ever, amen.

"Do you see how this passage not only affirms the Trinity—that is, that Christians worship one God who exists eternally as the three persons of the Father, Son, and Holy Ghost—but addresses an element of the faith that Christians still wrestle with: namely that we are saved through Christ to the glory of God, yet are called to do good works?"

"What about Ignatius?"

"Like Clement but with more rhetorical force, Ignatius fully affirms the God-man status of Jesus Christ as well as the physical reality of his incarnation, crucifixion, and resurrection. He even asserts clearly one of the key teachings of the New Testament and the Nicene Creed: that, as Paul himself affirms in 1 Corinthians 15, the risen Christ has a resurrection body, which he will retain for eternity. Or, to put that another way, the incarnation of Christ was not just for thirty-three years but forever.

"But here is the best part, the part that makes me so glad Stacey was able to find my book. In chapter 7 of his first epistle, the one to the Ephesians, Ignatius proclaims a majestic poem about Christ that most likely was an early Christian hymn. Listen to these eight lines of poetry that delve the depth of the mystery of Christ:

> Very flesh, yet Spirit too;
> Uncreated, and yet born;
> God-and-Man in One agreed,
> Very-Life-in-Death indeed,
> Fruit of God and Mary's seed;
> At once impassible and torn
> By pain and suffering here below:
> Jesus Christ, whom as our Lord we know.

"It's all there, the virgin birth, the incarnation, the deity of Christ, and in a letter written over two centuries before the Council of Nicaea."

"Can I see that passage?" said Bill.

I handed him the book and, as he read it over slowly, opened my mouth to say more. But the words never came out. Before I could utter a single syllable, a sound of jubilation rose up from the group around me.

The turkey had arrived!

SECOND COURSE

DINNER IS SERVED

4

DID THE RESURRECTION REALLY HAPPEN?

THE PROVIDERS OF THE TURKEY were two of my dearest friends in Houston. And what a turkey it was! Although Ali and his wife, Sara, were of Arabic descent and could do wonders with pita, kebabs, and hummus, they shared a love for French cuisine. For two whole days, they had marinated the turkey in a fine French wine, and then they had slow-cooked it for hours with onions and other spices. It was in fact their dedication to culinary excellence that had caused them to be late.

Because the turkey had been marinating in wine for so long, it had changed its color from brownish-white to a lovely shade of purple. All the guests immediately fell in love with the burgundy bird, and many pictures were taken of the prize turkey before we set ourselves to carving it up. After that, ten minutes of feverish activity ensued as the various and sundry dishes were arranged on the table, and the guests took their seats. Since my dining room table sat fourteen, we were all able to fit around it—barely.

Normally I would have said grace, but not this Thanksgiving. The nonagenarian founding father of my university, Stewart, was with us, and he had volunteered to offer the blessing. Stewart, who had fought in the eastern theater of World War II and had been close friends with Ali for many years, shared my love of history and would often sit in on my lectures for the honors college. As one of the key visionaries and architects of Houston Christian University, he had helped make HCU an urban hub where students from dozens of ethnic and religious backgrounds could come together and study the Great Books in a faithful but welcoming Christian environment.

It was that environment that had drawn me, a Northerner who had grown up in New Jersey and attended universities in New York and Michigan, to the great state of Texas. I could always elicit a smile from Stewart—a proud son of the South who owned one of the horse-drawn carriages used in *Gone with the Wind*—by assuring him that were it not for his crucial role in founding HCU, I would still be a Yankee!

In his prayer, Stewart not only blessed the food and the hands that had prepared it but thanked God for allowing us to live in a free country where folks like us could meet and converse in private without fearing that the Gestapo or the KGB or the CIA was monitoring our every word and action. Only in a land that guaranteed religious liberty and promoted free and open exchange between people of different cultures, convictions, and beliefs could we have enjoyed the kind of wide-ranging conversation that marked this as the most memorable Thanksgiving of my life.

Well, the most memorable . . . and the most exhausting.

I had barely begun to dive into my plate when Anthony, who had asked earlier about the virgin birth, raised another question about one specific miracle recorded in the Bible.

"Dr. Markos," he said, as he lifted a forkful of homemade mashed potatoes—my own contribution to the potluck—to his mouth, "I agreed with you when you said earlier that miracles don't break the laws of nature but merely suspend them. But I don't see how that argument holds for the resurrection. If I understand correctly, Christians don't just believe that Jesus' soul came back from the dead. They believe his body rose from the dead as well."

"That's absolutely right, Anthony. As crazy as it sounds, the Bible and the church both attest to Jesus' bodily resurrection from the dead. In fact, they teach something even crazier: that on the last day, our own bodies will be raised from the dead as well."

"But that's impossible. Dead cells and tissues can't magically regenerate. We *can* resuscitate people who have been dead for a short period of time, but not ones who are dead and buried. The kind of resurrection you describe does more than suspend the laws of nature; it defies them."

"Just before the turkey arrived, I read out loud a passage from Clement on the Trinity and on salvation. Do you remember?"

"Yes."

"Well, in chapter 25 of his epistle, Clement explains the Christian doctrine of the resurrection by comparing it to the phoenix."

"The phoenix?"

"The phoenix," said my son Alex, who could not help but break in at the mention of his favorite legend, "was a magical bird that lived for five hundred years. When the span of his life was over, the phoenix would build a fire, throw himself on it, and be consumed by the flames. Out of the ashes, a new phoenix would rise."

"But that is just a myth," said Anthony with a look of mild exasperation on his face. "Nothing in nature works like that!"

"Well, yes and no," I replied. "True, no one has ever seen an actual phoenix, but we have all seen an insect whose magical birth also parallels the doctrine of the resurrection. Does anyone know what insect I have in mind?"

"The butterfly," said Stacey.

"Exactly. The dull, earthbound caterpillar wraps itself in its own cocoon shroud, but that silken tomb becomes the chrysalis out of which the radiant butterfly emerges. We see something similar, do we not, in the transformation from acorn to oak tree? The hard, brittle acorn is buried in the ground, where it lies cold and dead, but out of that dry corpse there emerges the glorious tree whose branches reach for the heavens.

"Of course, the butterfly and the oak offer only faint glimpses of what is to come. According to the Bible, nature is as fallen as we are. Sin has caused our world to be subjected to decay and futility, but a time is coming when all will be restored.

"Anthony, am I correct in saying that our body *should* be able to regenerate dead nerve and brain cells?"

"Well yes, I suppose so. Our body created them in the first place, and there are cells in our body, like skin cells, that do regenerate."

"So why do people die of old age?"

"It's hard to say. It's as if the body just starts shutting itself down."

"Anthony, the Bible proclaims, and science has shown, that we are fearfully and wonderfully made. Our bodies are amazingly complex, and that complexity goes all the way down to the microscopic level, to the molecular machines that help to replicate the DNA and to carry out the code stored within it."

"That is true, but I don't see what you're getting at."

"What I'm trying to say is that our bodies possess the blueprints, the structures, and the energies to repair themselves endlessly—but they don't. Even if we don't get into an accident or contract a fatal disease, the fuel eventually runs out and the factory shuts down. There seems to be a flaw in the system, without which we could stay young and healthy for a very long time."

"Dad," said Stacey, "I hope you are not thinking about getting a toupee."

"No, no," I laughed, rubbing my right hand across my mostly naked scalp, "I have embraced my male-pattern baldness. But your question, Stacey, raises an important point.

"Anthony, you are still a young man, but I'll bet if you asked all the people here who, like myself, have passed their fiftieth year whether they felt any different than they did when they were twenty, they would tell you that they did not.

"What do you think?" I said, gazing around the table at my fellow fifty-plus-ers. Though no one spoke out loud, I could tell by their faces that they agreed.

"Now," I continued, "I'm not saying that we don't feel a few more aches and pains in our bodies; still, we never quite accept our age as a thing that should have dominion over us. My mother once told me that she sometimes thought she had only dreamed that she had had kids and that they had grown up and moved away and started families of their own. I thought that a bit strange when she first said it to me, but now that I have two grown kids, with one working down in San Antonio and the other about to graduate from college, I know exactly what she meant. The old saying that you are only as old as you feel is more than a sentimental cliché.

"None of us is immune from a little vanity about our appearance, but that does not take away from our universal, unshakable sense that time and age and the slow decay of our bodies and minds are somehow alien to us. They should not control us the way they do. We weren't made for this world of entropy, in which the rose withers and the morning glory fades, where time's winged chariot ever hastens on, where nothing gold can stay. We were made for eternity, for a perpetual present where it is always *now*, always today. There is something within all of us that defies the tyranny of time."

"Dad," said Alex, "tell them about the remote control."

"Thanks for reminding me, Alex," I said and then cast my gaze again around the table. "I like to tell my kids that one of our greatest intimations of heaven is the remote control. But before I tell you why, I'd like to share with you a historical fact that very few people know: My father was the first person in America to have a remote control."

"Really?" said several people at once.

"Yes. It was called 'me'!"

I paused for a few seconds to allow a mutual groan to circle the table.

"But seriously," I continued, "the remote control is a magical device. It provides us with a twenty-foot arm. That may seem to have nothing to do with heaven, but I think it does. Just as we never quite accept the limits that time and age impose on us, so most of us rebel in one way or another against the tyranny of space. We feel, even if we never put it into words, that the barriers of time and space are finally artificial, that they should not have the power to imprison us as they do.

"Now I'm not saying that this deep-seated feeling, this refusal to fully accept our spatiotemporal limits, offers categorical proof of the resurrection, but I do believe it reveals that the Christian doctrine that Jesus rose bodily from the dead and that we will someday do so as well is neither as irrational nor as foreign as it might at first appear."

As I finished, Anthony smiled and nodded, but Bill looked decidedly unconvinced.

"Now wait a minute," Bill broke in, "I grant that what you just said is quite moving and that it possesses a strong emotional appeal and imaginative force. Nevertheless, it doesn't give me any reason to believe that the resurrection of Jesus actually happened."

"You are right," I admitted. "It does not. The fact that we yearn to transcend the boundaries of time and space does not prove that we will actually do so. But it should make us more willing to approach the Bible's claim that Jesus rose from the dead as one that, were it true, would provide the answer to one of our deepest desires."

"Granted, but what proof is there that it took place?"

"Remember what we said before the turkey arrived. The Gospels, whether or not we believe them to be directly inspired by God, are reliable historical documents. As such, they all record a simple fact of history: that when the women came to the tomb on Easter morning to anoint the body of Jesus, the tomb was empty."

"Who's to say that grave robbers did not break in to the tomb?"

"That's a good suggestion, but it has two problems. First, the tomb was guarded by Roman soldiers and was covered by a very large stone. Second, even if the robbers could have eluded the guards and broken in, they would not have stolen the body and left the grave clothes. It was the grave clothes, not the body, that was worth money."

"Well, maybe it was the Pharisees or the Romans that stole it."

"That sounds a bit more convincing, but it smacks up against another problem. The new Christian sect rested firmly and securely on the disciples' claim that Jesus had risen bodily from the dead. The Pharisees, who opposed the new church, could have strangled Christianity in its crib by producing the body. The Romans could have done the same, either by producing it themselves or by selling it to the Pharisees. Now that I think of it, if the first scenario were true and grave robbers had stolen the body, then they too could have sold it to the Pharisees for a very high price."

"But what about the disciples themselves? Surely they would have a good motive to steal the body."

"Yes, I think that is the most logical scenario, but it too runs up against a major obstacle. All the disciples but John, who was exiled, died martyr deaths on account of their faith in the risen Christ. History offers many examples of people willing to die for something they believe in strongly, even if that something turns out to be false. But people do not die for something they *know* is a hoax.

"You see, if the disciples had stolen the body, then they would have known that Christ did not rise from the dead and that not only was their faith false in terms of its claims but that it lacked the power to save them from their sins. Paul himself admitted that if Christ did not rise from the dead, then the Christian faith is futile, and we are without hope in this world or the next (1 Cor 15:12-19)."

"Well, maybe they hallucinated the resurrection."

"It's possible that one person might have experienced a hallucination, but not all of them. The records testify to multiple appearances in which the risen Christ appeared to numerous disciples at different times and in different places. It is not psychologically tenable for a large number of people to all experience the same hallucination, especially when they are not expecting it and don't believe it when they see it."

"How do you mean?"

"When Christ appeared to his disciples, they did not immediately believe it. They thought he was a ghost and were afraid to draw near to him. Jesus himself had to reassure them that he had indeed risen bodily from the dead by inviting them to touch his body and by eating food with them (Lk 24:37-43)."

"Didn't the Jews of Jesus' day believe in the resurrection of the body?"

"They did, but they all thought it would happen at the end of the world. That's why, when Martha tells Jesus that her brother Lazarus would not have died had he been there, and Jesus tells her that Lazarus will rise again, Martha says that she knows he will rise again at the last day (Jn 11:24). Can anyone tell me how Jesus responded?"

David, who had been listening carefully to the conversation from the other side of the table, jumped in to supply the answer: "He told her that he was the resurrection and the life and that anyone who believed in him would never die (Jn 11:25)."

"Yes, yes," I said, "that beautiful promise is recited at most Christian funerals to remind us that our faith in the resurrection of the dead rests on the reality of Jesus' resurrection on that first Easter morning."

"I don't know," said Bill, after thinking a bit. "It all sounds a bit legendary to me. You said earlier that Christ could only have been a liar, a lunatic, or the Lord. But isn't there a fourth possible *l* word? What if he was merely a legend?"

"That's a good question that has been raised quite often over the last three hundred years. Surely history bears testimony to such legends; my favorite is the one that says King Arthur is not dead but is sleeping on the isle of Avalon, awaiting the day when the world needs him again. But this does not apply to Jesus for at least two reasons. The first reason, as we have seen, is that the birth, death, and resurrection of Jesus are fully grounded in history."

"What is the second?"

"It takes a long time for legends to form and develop. The resurrection of Jesus is attested to immediately as a historical fact; it doesn't take shape slowly over decades."

"But you admitted earlier that about a generation passed from the death of Jesus to the first written Gospel."

"Thirty years is not enough time for a legend as far-ranging as the resurrection to be invented. Besides, Matthew and John were eyewitnesses to the resurrection, and Luke and Mark interviewed eyewitnesses when they wrote their own Gospels. But, beyond that, we have an even earlier testimony to the resurrection."

"Who is that?"

"Paul. Most scholars, Christian or otherwise, date 1 Corinthians to the 50s AD. Here is what Paul writes in 1 Corinthians 15:

> For I delivered to you as of first importance what I also received: that Christ died for our sins in accordance with the Scriptures, that he was buried, that he was raised on the third day in accordance with the Scriptures, and that he appeared to Cephas [Peter], then to the twelve. Then he appeared to more than

> five hundred brothers at one time, most of whom are still alive, though some have fallen asleep. Then he appeared to James, then to all the apostles. Last of all, as to one untimely born, he appeared also to me. (1 Cor 15:3-8)

"But that was written twenty-five years after the event."

"It was, but note how Paul introduces the passage. He says that he is delivering to us what he received from others. That is formal language, Bill, that was used in Paul's day to indicate that someone had received and was formally transmitting the oral tradition that had been entrusted to him."

"Oh, you mean like the telephone game!"

"I know that people often use that analogy when talking about oral tradition, but that is not how things worked in the time of Christ. The passing down of tradition was a sacred trust that was taken very seriously and possessed a high degree of accuracy. *Tradition* in Latin means, literally, 'to hand down or give over.' Paul was a Pharisee, and they, like the scribes, were people who held tradition in the highest esteem. Since we know that Paul visited the church at Jerusalem just a year or two after the death of Christ, the tradition he here passes down likely dates to just a few years after the event!"

"I must admit that's impressive."

"I do believe it is, Bill. Note that what Paul passes down is not an indistinct or poetic legend but a list of actual people who saw the risen Christ—a list that could have been checked and verified. It is also a list that includes three very different eyewitnesses whose lives were radically changed by their encounter with the resurrected Jesus."

"Who do you mean?"

"The first is Peter, a disciple who denied Jesus and ran away. And yet, something happened to him that transformed him from a coward to a bold leader and martyr whom Catholics consider to be the first pope. James, the brother of Jesus was at first an unbeliever in the deity of Christ (Jn 7:5). Yet something happened to him that turned him into a follower of Jesus who led the church in Jerusalem and died a martyr's death. Finally, Paul himself was a highly educated Pharisee who fiercely persecuted the church until something convinced him to become a Christian missionary who took the gospel as far as Rome and died as a martyr for the religion he had once sought to destroy.

"Indeed, when the resurrected Christ appeared to the disciples in the upper room, they were defeated and terrified. They had all scattered during the crucifixion and were now huddled together in fear of their lives (Jn 20:19). Then something happened that transformed them into bold witnesses and martyrs. Only one event can explain the drastic shift in Peter, James, Paul, and the disciples. They all, at different times and places, had encountered the risen Christ: a fact attested to by their changed lives and by an oft-overlooked detail, that all the sermons in Acts rest on the disciples' proclamation that they are witnesses of the resurrection (Acts 2:32; 3:15; 5:30-32; 10:39-41; 13:29-31)."

"You make a strong case here, but I noticed something odd about the passage from Paul that you just read."

"What's that?"

"Paul doesn't say anything about Mary Magdalene and the other women going to the tomb and finding Jesus' body gone."

"Wow, Bill, you have an excellent eye—and ear—for detail! Not many readers pick up on that. I certainly didn't myself until it was pointed out to me. But that slight discrepancy actually strengthens the case for the resurrection. It shows how quickly the church leaders tried to tidy up that embarrassing detail."

"Why embarrassing?"

"Because in Jesus' day women's testimony was not admissible in court."

"Then why do the Gospels all say that the women were the first witnesses?"

"Bill, you have hit on one of the strongest proofs that the Gospels are based on eyewitness accounts. There is only one possible reason why all four Gospels would present Mary and the other women as the first witnesses of the resurrection."

"What reason is that?"

"That that is what actually happened. Had the Gospel writers been trying to make up a false story to back up their claim that Jesus had risen, they would not have told it the way they did. They would have had one of the male disciples or, better yet, a Jewish leader like Nicodemus or Joseph of Arimathea be the first to see the risen Christ."

"Good point, but don't the accounts of the resurrection in the four Gospels differ in their details?"

"They do, but please remember what we said about the Gospels before dinner. Their reliability in the court of history rests precisely on the fact that the accounts complement rather than simply repeat one another. If the accounts of the resurrection were wildly different, they would lose their credibility. But they would also lose their credibility if they were identical. Had the accounts mimicked each other word for word and detail for detail, that would suggest that the early church had colluded in fashioning an airtight story. Instead, we get what the Gospels claim to offer: separate, eyewitness-based accounts of the same event that work together to paint an accurate and reliable 'crime scene' for the resurrection."

Bill was about to respond when Sita, who had been thinking very deeply for the last ten minutes, broke in.

"Dr. Markos," she said in a quiet voice, "everything you say makes sense, but I don't see why it matters whether the resurrection actually happened."

Though many of the guests were taken aback by Sita's question, I, knowing her Hindu background, was not too surprised.

"Sita," I asked, "are you thinking about the stories of Vishnu, about how he entered our world and then left it in a number of different guises?"

"Yes," she answered, relieved that I could see where she was coming from. "My religion teaches that Vishnu came to earth in various avatars or incarnations—not just the human forms of Rama and Krishna but as a fish, a turtle, a boar, and a man-lion—and then returned to the divine, heavenly realms."

"Yes, that is what I was thinking. But tell me, Sita, are those events historical?"

"Not really," she answered. "What is important about those stories is not when, or even whether, they happened in the literal sense of the word. All that matters is the message behind the story, that the gods are close to us and that they understand the mess our world is in."

"Back in the 1940s and '50s, a German theologian named Rudolf Bultmann set himself the task of demythologizing the supernatural claims of the Gospels. He argued that the historical details weren't important, only the kernels of truth to be mined from the stories. He taught what Bill suggested a moment ago, that the stories surrounding Christ are best treated as legendary. In many ways, Sita, his work reflects what you just said about Hinduism. The truth of the religion does not rest on whether Vishnu literally incarnated himself as Rama or Krishna at a specific time and place in history."

"Yes, that is true. But why isn't it the same for Christianity?"

"Because in Christianity, it is not the story that saves but the reality. The disciples did not preach that the resurrection was a spiritual parable to reflect and meditate on. They claimed, on the basis of evidence they saw with their own eyes and touched with their own hands, that Jesus had literally conquered the power of death when he rose bodily from the grave.

"No one bothers to date the avatars of Vishnu or the various tales told by the ancient Greeks and Romans, for they are not historical events. But Jesus died and rose in the city of Jerusalem while Tiberius was emperor, Pontius Pilate was Roman procurator, and Herod Antipas was the Jewish king.

"Sita, if I were to go to a devout Hindu and prove to him that Krishna was not an actual historical person who lived at a specific time and in a specific place, do you think that would cause him to abandon his faith?"

"No, I don't think so. It would not take away from the spiritual truth that is the real center of his belief."

"What if someone could prove to me that Christ did not rise from the dead on that first Easter morning? What impact do you think that would have on me?"

"I'm not sure."

"It would completely destroy my faith. Oh, I could go on trying to live my life by some of the teachings of Jesus, but I could no longer call myself a true believer, for to be a Christian is to rest one's faith on a literal savior who rose from the dead. If Jesus is still in the grave, then I have no reason to believe that he was who he claimed to be, or that my sins are forgiven, or that Christ is now in heaven preparing a place for me and for all those who put their faith in him."

"Is it really as all-or-nothing as that?"

"It is. A moment ago, I mentioned that Paul treated the resurrection as the central, nonnegotiable event in the history of Christianity. I think it's worth my reading aloud his shocking statement: 'If Christ has not been raised, then our preaching is in vain and your faith is in vain. We are even found to be misrepresenting God, because we testified about God that he raised Christ. . . . If Christ has not been raised, your faith is futile and you are still in your sins. . . . If in Christ we have hope in this life only, we are of all people most to be pitied' (1 Cor 15:14-15, 17, 19)."

"He doesn't leave much wiggle room, does he?"

"No, Sita, he doesn't. Christianity rises or falls on a literal, historical resurrection. Had the Pharisees or Romans been able to produce the body of Jesus, they would have strangled Christianity in its cradle. The disciples knew this; that is why they did not cease to proclaim the resurrection as the center of their faith and their hope. Indeed, when they met to discuss who would take the place of Judas the traitor, Peter made it clear that Judas's replacement would have to be someone who could 'become with us a witness to his resurrection' (Acts 1:22).

"For many people today," I continued, lifting my gaze to take in all the guests at the table, "Christianity has become an emotional, feel-good religion with little grounding in reason, logic, and science. That is a kind of Christianity the believers of the early, medieval, and Reformation churches would not have recognized. They knew Christianity rested on rational, historical claims that were either true or false. When a Christian says that Christ rose again on Easter, he does not mean that he can feel Christ's love and goodness in his heart or that the idea of resurrection resonates with his spirit. He means, simply and literally, that Jesus of Nazareth rose bodily from the grave."

"But why is such a thing necessary to achieve salvation? And why, in any case, would a man seeking salvation and spiritual enlightenment want to retain his body?"

The question came from a middle-aged woman seated across from me at the table; she was a practicing Buddhist from China whom Ali had invited and who went by the American name of Elaine. Only yesterday, Elaine had completed a silent retreat at a temple in Houston, and the peace and serenity of her experience still clung to her.

5

WHAT IS THE REAL PROBLEM WITH MAN?

IT IS A SAD BUT MOSTLY ACCURATE TRUTH that whereas a person who speaks three languages is called trilingual and a person who speaks two languages is called bilingual, a person who speaks only one language is called an American. In sharp contrast to us poor monolingual citizens of the United Sates, my friend Ali was, if I may coin a new word, pentalingual! In addition to mastering English, Arabic, French, and Spanish, Ali had taught himself Chinese.

Though his knowledge of the language spoken by over one billion people was initially tied to his business concerns, he had grown increasingly interested in the aesthetic, philosophical, culinary, and religious culture of China. Through him, I was afforded the pleasure of meeting dozens of Chinese people from various religious backgrounds and from all areas of that vast Middle Kingdom that has fascinated and puzzled Westerners for thousands of years.

While Ali preferred the purely philosophical branches of Chinese Buddhism that focused on achieving a proper balance in all things—he was a student of the ancient *I Ching* or *Book of Changes*—Elaine took very seriously the religious aspects of her faith, including its belief in reincarnation. She was a gentle, soft-spoken woman who spent much time in meditation. I had learned a great deal from her about the Chinese soul and its unique perspective on God, man, and the universe.

As I filled my plate with a second round of food, I mused silently on the best way to address Elaine's questions about salvation and the resurrection of the body. For her questions, though seemingly simple on the surface, pointed to a major distinction between the foundational assumptions of Buddhism and Hinduism, on the one hand, and Judaism, Christianity, and Islam, on the other.

"Elaine," I said, "I am so glad you are here with us today and that you asked those questions. Whether you realize it or not, your questions cut to the heart of a fundamental difference between the teachings of Buddha and those of Christ and the Bible."

"What difference is that?"

"That the two religions offer a radically different answer and solution to the same essential, underlying question: What is the problem with man?"

"The problem with man?"

"What is it that prevents us from being the people we know we can be? Why is it that everything we build eventually goes bad and falls apart? What's *wrong* with us?"

"According to Buddha," said Elaine, "the road to enlightenment begins with the knowledge that life is filled with pain and disease and death."

"Yes, that is true, but that only describes the condition of the world in which we find ourselves. Pain and disease and death are all inescapable realities. But what role do *we* play in all of that? What is the problem with man, with us human beings who must live in a world of leprosy and war and bitter old age?"

"Desire. It is our desires that turn us aside from the true path."

"Do you mean good desires or bad desires?"

"*All* desires: Clinging to any desire ties us down and prevents our soul from freeing itself from the illusions of this world."

"Elaine, if I may put that thought on hold for a moment, I would like to ask Ali to tell us a story that he has shared with me many times before. It is the true story of the unique childhood and education of the Buddha. Ali, would you like to tell us the story of Siddhartha Gautama and how he became the Buddha?"

"Certainly! Siddhartha was born in the sixth century before Christ, a full hundred years before Plato. His rich father swore that he would shield his princely son from all pain, disease, and death. As a result, the young man who would become the Buddha lived a life of pure pleasure, never setting his eyes on the sorrows of poverty or age or sickness. He did not even know that such a thing as death existed!"

I could tell by the expressions on the faces of my dinner guests that they were as mesmerized by Ali's story as I had been the first time he had told it to me. Siddhartha's father had conducted a strange experiment indeed on his unsuspecting son. But what would be the upshot of his experiment?

"Although Prince Siddhartha had everything," Ali continued, "including a beautiful wife who bore him a son, he felt empty inside, for his life had no meaning or purpose. Finally, against the commands of his father, he left his sheltered paradise to see his subjects who lived outside the palace walls. On four successive trips, he met an old man, a sick man, a decaying corpse, and an ascetic. Impressed by the fourth, he abandoned his family and his princedom for the life of a wandering beggar. At first, he adopted a severe ascetic lifestyle, living, they say, on one grain of rice a day. But, in the end, he adopted a middle way between asceticism and indulgence."

"Thank you, Ali," I said. "I never get tired of hearing that amazing story."

"That story," said Elaine, "is one of the things that attracted me to Buddhism. I have always been impressed by Siddhartha's renunciation of his wealth and power."

"I'm not sure if you are aware of it," I said, addressing the table as a whole, "but one of the most famous medieval Christians had an upbringing similar to Siddhartha and made a similar decision when he reached adulthood. He was born in Italy in 1181 to a wealthy silk merchant; though his given name was Giovanni, his father called him Francesco. Young Francesco was given all that money could buy, and he indulged his passions for love, wine, fine clothes, and military honor. But an illness and a term in prison sobered him up and forced him to reevaluate his empty, purposeless life. In the end, he stripped himself naked before his father and the town of Assisi, abandoned his possessions, married himself to Lady Poverty, and became a wandering friar."

"Assisi!" exclaimed Stacey, who had visited the city with the honors college a year earlier. "You must be telling the story of Saint Francis of Assisi."

"I am! Like Siddhartha, Saint Francis chose the way of total renunciation, taking the monastic vows of poverty, chastity, and obedience. But instead of rejecting the world, with all its desires and illusions, he started a new order of friars that served the poor, the sick, and the homeless and that helped purify the church of its worldly excesses."

"Are you suggesting that Francis was a better man than the Buddha?"

"No, no, not at all. Both were men of compassion and vision who taught a new and better way to their followers. But the Buddha, who grew up as a Hindu, did not try to change the world the way Francis did because his answer to our initial question—what is the problem with man?—differed radically from that of Francis. A moment ago, Elaine, you gave that problem a name."

"I did. The problem is desire. But wouldn't Francis have agreed with that?"

"No, Francis would have said the problem was sin."

"But aren't *desire* and *sin* two ways of saying the same thing?"

"No, sin is not another name for desire. The problem is not that we have desires or even that we act on them but that our desires are misdirected."

"If that is true, then isn't the best way to remedy that misdirection to eliminate desire altogether?"

"So it would seem, but not if those desires were put inside of us by the God who created us. Elaine, have you ever been troubled by the fact that the same human race can produce good, kind men like Francis and the Buddha and evil, tyrannical men like Adolf Hitler and Joseph Stalin?"

"Isn't that just the way of things?"

"I suppose so, but only because we have gotten used to things being that way. We have also forgotten that there is something even more peculiar about our species: Every single one of us has a little Buddha and a little Hitler fighting within him. Why is it that we are capable of such love and self-sacrifice and yet such hatred and anger?"

"Isn't the problem desire?"

"I don't think so, for our desires push us toward both good things and bad things. The same desire for physical love can lead a man to a faithful marriage or to a life of sexual license. The desire itself is neutral; it is how we channel the desire that makes the difference. So it is with a knife: A surgeon uses it to heal, while a thief uses it to murder."

"But how can that be? How can good and evil be so closely intertwined?"

"Elaine, the first thing that attracted me to the Bible was that it gave me the only satisfactory answer I have found to that most puzzling of questions. According to Genesis, God created us, our world, and our desires as good things, but we disobeyed him and sought our own good outside God's will for us. The only explanation I have found that can account for our dual capacity for virtue and vice is that we were created good in the image of God but that we have fallen away from him into sin and rebellion."

"I think there is another explanation, one that also makes sense of our conflicting desires: The soul and its desires are good, while the body and its desires are evil."

As I pondered Elaine's suggestion, I unconsciously scanned my eyes around the room. In addition to leading the international Bible study at my home, I had taught an English as a Second Language Bible study on my university campus that included many students from China and Japan. Because those countries place a high premium on gift giving, I had received many Japanese and Chinese rice-paper prints that I had hung on the walls of the dining room.

Some of those prints included lovely ladies holding parasols; others included tigers; yet others were adorned with bamboo shoots and fans. As I tried to formulate a response to Elaine, my eyes fell on one print that boasted a yin and yang at its center.

"Listen, everyone," I said, as I reached for another helping of turkey, mashed potatoes, and stuffing, "Elaine has just offered a suggestion that has great relevance to the international makeup of our Thanksgiving dinner!"

Once I had managed to gather everyone's attention around the table, I continued: "Friends, Elaine has just put her finger on something comparative religion teachers often hold up as a defining distinction between the religions of the West and of the East. They are both right and wrong to do so."

"What distinction do you have in mind?" asked Elaine, who was a bit puzzled as to why I had been so excited by her suggestion.

"Elaine, there are two basic ways to explain why good and evil stand side by side in our world and ourselves. One way is to say that we were created good but are fallen. The other way is to say that there is a good and bad principle fighting it out inside us."

"That's what the great Persian prophet Zoroaster taught," said Reza, seeming shocked and pleased that I would reference the original religion of Iran.

"Yes, Reza, Zoroaster—or Zarathustra, as he is sometimes called in the West—taught that our soul stands on a bridge while the forces of good and evil pull us in opposite directions. Although there are very few people today who believe literally in Zoroaster's powerful image, millions of people throughout history have accepted a dualistic view of the world."

"What do you mean by *dualism*?"

"Dualism, Reza, is the belief that there are two competing powers or entities or principles in the world. For Zoroaster, that duality took the form of a good god and a bad god warring for our soul. For Taoists, dualism is embodied in the image and concept of yin and yang. But for most dualistic thinkers, the two principles at war are the soul and the body: or, to put it in more philosophical terms, mind and matter. Elaine's suggestion that the soul and its desires are good while the body and its desires are bad embodies a dualistic explanation for why things are the way they are."

"But what does that have to do with what you just said about East and West?"

"Thank you for reminding me, Reza! Sometimes I get so excited by conversations like this one that I forget the initial point I wanted to make. Today, religious people who privilege the soul over the body and who therefore try to transcend the flesh and the material world tend to be Hindus or Buddhists from the East, or Western New Agers who look to the East for spiritual direction.

"That, at least, is the common view. As it turns out, dualism was very strong in the Greek Plato and in the Neoplatonic thinkers that came after him. It also undergirded the various Gnostic groups that, during the early centuries of Christianity, denied the incarnation as both blasphemous and foolish. Think about it: If the body and matter are inherently bad, then how could God have taken on human flesh without subjecting himself to evil?"

"But if dualism was so strong in the West, why did the West abandon it?"

"Because of Christianity, because the church taught that matter and the flesh are inherently good, so good that God himself entered into both. The great philosopher and theologian who helped Christians understand this was Saint Augustine. After spending many years as a Neoplatonist and a Gnostic, he finally found his way into the church."

"But, if I may ask," said Elaine, "why does Christianity think it is wrong to say that the soul is good and the body bad?"

"Well, though I hate to admit it, there are a very large number of Christians in this country who are dualists without realizing it. In churches across America, people think that the goal of Christianity is to leave the body behind and become pure spirit. That is why so many Christians think that when we die, we become angels."

"Dr. Markos," said David, "are you thinking about *It's a Wonderful Life*?"

"You have a good memory, David," I said and turned to address the entire table. "Many years ago, David took a class I taught on the films of Frank Capra. Capra's most famous film, and the best Christmas movie ever made, is *It's a Wonderful Life*. Though the movie affirms Christian values, it unfortunately perpetuates the myth that angels are the souls of people who have died."

"But isn't that what Christianity teaches?" said Reza and Elaine together.

"No, despite popular opinion, neither Christ nor the Bible nor Christianity has ever taught that. Angels and humans are different creations of God. Angels are pure spirit, but not human beings. We are physical and spiritual. The promise that has always lain at the heart of Christianity is that in heaven we, like Jesus himself, will have resurrection bodies and will dwell for eternity in a physical place that the Bible calls the new Jerusalem. Now, that place will be physical in a perfected way we cannot imagine, but it will nevertheless be physical.

"By the way, Elaine, I wonder if you've noticed that I have finally gotten around to addressing your initial question about why a man in search of salvation and spiritual enlightenment would want to retain his body."

"Yes, I did notice, but I'm not sure I'm clear yet on the answer."

"I just said a moment ago that Plato was a dualist, but that is not the only thing he has in common with Hindus and Buddhists. Though Western readers are often shocked to discover it, Plato, like Pythagoras before him, taught the transmigration of the soul."

"Plato believed in reincarnation?"

"He did, but that part of his philosophical system was abandoned when the West adopted Christianity. Plato could believe in reincarnation because he had a low view of the body; he saw it as nothing more than a prison house of the soul, something to be discarded after it had served its purpose."

"But I don't see what's wrong with that. Isn't the body the thing that weighs us down? Doesn't salvation mean escaping the body and the material world?"

"Elaine, you suggested that the soul and its desires are good, and the body and its desires are bad. But is that really the case? The worst sins of all, greed and pride and envy and hypocrisy, come not from our body but from our soul. The sins we commit with our flesh are minor compared to those that proceed from our soul. The SS soldiers who served Hitler lived physically pure lives; they did not drink or smoke or sleep around. But their souls were filled with malice and rage toward their enemies.

"Once Augustine was able to move away from Neoplatonism and Gnosticism to embrace the incarnation, crucifixion, and resurrection of Christ, he took a second, more careful look at the nature of good and evil. What he discovered was that evil is not a thing at all but the lack or perversion of a thing."

"You'll have to explain that a bit more," said Elaine.

"Good and evil are not separate but equal powers, nor does one inhere in the soul and the other in the body. Evil is not a positive thing at all but a falling away from goodness. God made all things good: body and soul, matter and mind, reason and desire. But when we disobeyed God, those good things went bad. Cut off from the God who created them and filled them with their proper purpose, they went astray and fell into corruption. Imagine if I didn't know the true purpose and design of my piano. If I didn't know it was meant to make music, I might use it as a battering ram and thus destroy it and its true potential."

"So salvation for a Christian," said Elaine slowly and thoughtfully, "doesn't mean escaping from the body and the world?"

"No, it is not about leaving flesh and matter behind but about redeeming and restoring both to their original purity and purpose. For Christians, Jesus is both the Son of God and the second Adam. When he died on the cross, he took on himself the punishment for our sins, but he did something else as well. By being perfectly obedient to his Father, even to the point of a humiliating and painful death, Jesus took back the disobedience of Adam. He set right what had been broken."

"But I still think it is a better and more spiritual thing to leave the world behind."

"The Gnostics believed something that parallels many of the ancient assumptions that underlie Hinduism and Buddhism. According to the Bible, God created the world good, but it fell into sin and corruption; according to the Gnostics, it was creation itself that was the fall. Some even taught that physical matter was the aborted creation of a lesser god. That is why they believed that true salvation meant escaping from matter."

"But how can the soul be free if it is still chained to flesh and matter?"

"Because it is not physical matter that is the problem. Flesh and soul are equally fallen into sin; both have gone astray, following misdirected desires that cause them both to decay and grow corrupt. Just as there is some real good in our soul, so there is real good in our body. Our soul needs to be redeemed, renewed, and restored to its original state, and the same goes for our body. And not just our body but our desires as well."

"I see you've led us back to desire again."

"I'm sorry if I seem to be repeating myself, but desire really does lie at the crux of the matter. If all desires deceive and lead astray, then Buddha was right to reject them. But if our desires were originally good, if God placed them in us so that we might seek after him, then desire, far from impeding salvation, is central to achieving it."

"But desire is too strong, too loud, too . . . discordant. One cannot achieve true enlightenment in the presence of desire."

"There are many Christians who might say the same, but I would suggest, along with C. S. Lewis, that the problem with our desires is not that they are too strong for heaven but that they are too weak."

"Dad," said Alex, "do you want me to get your copy of *The Weight of Glory*?"

"Thanks, Alex, but there's no need," I said. "I love that Lewis sermon so much that I have committed the passage you have in mind to memory.

"Friends," I continued, deepening my voice slightly and lifting my hands for dramatic effect, "I'd like to share with you one of my favorite quotes from C. S. Lewis. The topic is the role that joy and desire play in our journey toward God and heaven: 'We are half-hearted creatures, fooling about with drink and sex and ambition when infinite joy is offered us, like an ignorant child who wants to go on making mud pies in a slum because he cannot imagine what is meant by the offer of a holiday at the sea. We are far too easily pleased.'

"Many people, Christians included, think that the problem with lust and gluttony and avarice is that they are so strong that they will shatter the peace and equanimity of heaven. The real problem is quite the opposite. Lust and gluttony and avarice are too weak and feeble to survive the thundering joy and ecstasy of heaven."

"Thanks, Dr. Markos," said Sita, "for sharing that. I've always felt that there is something overly masculine about Hinduism and Buddhism in their purest form. I know that my desires and emotions and feelings have often gotten me into trouble, but I've never been able to believe that eliminating them would make things better."

"That's a good point, Sita. I've noticed that the temptation to rigidly control one's emotions is stronger in men than in women. Many a wife has had to convince her husband that emotions are not always negative, that it is okay to let one's feelings out. But, Sita, you seem to want to say something else."

"As a matter of fact, I do have another question that's been on the tip of my tongue for the last ten minutes. In Hinduism and Buddhism, the real problem is not sin or even desire: It's ignorance. Salvation means having the blinders taken away from your eyes so that you can see the real nature of reality. In the *Gita*, as we discussed earlier, that happens when Arjuna suddenly realizes that all is one, that Brahman is atman."

"Sita, I wish all my students were as thoughtful and studious as you. Just as Elaine put her finger on a key issue when she suggested the soul is good and the body is bad, so you have put your finger on the other key issue in the ongoing conversation about what the real problem with man is."

"I have?"

"Yes, and quite succinctly! Alex, can you please tell us all what the word *Gnostic* means in Greek."

"Sure. *Gnostic* comes from the Greek verb for knowing. A Gnostic is a 'knower.'"

"Excellent! Your Greek and Latin professors taught you well! Sita, another thing Gnostics have in common with most Hindus and Buddhists is that they believed that salvation comes not from having our sins atoned for but from the possession of secret wisdom known only to those in the group. That is why the Gnostic Gospels don't have Jesus do anything historical; he just passes on a number of wise sayings, the kind you might read in the *Analects* of Confucius or the teachings of Buddha."

"What do you mean when you say Jesus doesn't do anything historical?"

"Because the problem is seen to be ignorance rather than sin, the Gnostic Jesus needs only to open our eyes, to enlighten us with truths hidden from the common man. He doesn't have to perform miracles or die and rise again. Like Buddha, the Gnostic Jesus is a teacher committed to instructing; neither is a savior committed to rescuing and redeeming us from our sin."

"*Buddha*," said Elaine, "means 'enlightened one.' Anyone who follows the noble path laid down by Siddhartha can achieve enlightenment and thus become a Buddha."

"Thanks for that clarification: Etymologically speaking, to become a Buddha one must be a Gnostic! I think the best way I can sum up the belief that sin is ignorance and therefore salvation can only come from enlightenment is by quoting a line from a British poet and artist named William Blake, who was quite Gnostic in outlook and who wrote many cryptic poems filled with esoteric insights. In one of those poems, he wrote, 'If the doors of perception were cleansed everything would appear to man as it is, infinite. For man has closed himself up, till he sees all things thro' narrow chinks of his cavern.'"

"That sounds very Buddhist," said Elaine.

"It does, and, as such it helps remind us that the differences we see in religion do not always represent a simple dichotomy between East and West. If ignorance is indeed the root problem, then that truth is true whether we live in America or China, England or India. Likewise, if the problem is sin, then that truth equally cuts across all ethnic and national boundaries. People in all parts of the world have in their own way wrestled with the sin-versus-ignorance question. In fact, you might be surprised to know that even within the Judeo-Christian framework of the West, that question has been the cause of much religious, philosophical, and political debate."

"That is surprising," said Sita, "though I seem to recall you mentioning something about that debate in one of your classes."

"You have a good memory! I mentioned the debate during a lecture on the legacy of the French Revolution. Influenced by the writings of Jean-Jacques Rousseau, the architects of that world-changing event decided to discard the traditional biblical belief that the problem with man is sin and disobedience. They argued instead that the real problem with man is ignorance and poverty. Eliminate those, and you can build utopia."

"If I remember correctly," said Sita, "their utopia did not turn out so well."

"It certainly did not; it led to injustice, tyranny, unlawful seizures of property, and mass killing. And the same thing has happened again and again: in the Russia of Lenin and Stalin, the Germany of Hitler, the Cambodia of Pol Pot, the China of Mao Zedong, and the Cuba of Fidel Castro."

"Why do you think that is?"

"Because, Sita, ignorance is not the real problem. The problem is not that we don't know what is right and what is wrong. The problem is that we do know and yet choose the wrong path anyway. Now, I believe we should do all that we can to alleviate ignorance and poverty—Christianity, in fact, has the best record of doing just that—but that's not where the real problem lies. Plato, as brilliant as he was, often taught that virtue is knowledge: that is to say, if we truly understood virtue, we would practice it. The more realistic, pragmatic Aristotle knew better. The very thing that makes vice, vice is that we know a thing is wrong and yet do it nonetheless. If we were truly ignorant, then we would not be guilty. But, 95 percent of the time, we are not ignorant."

"But why," asked Sita, "does a belief that the problem with man is ignorance lead to mass purges? I don't see the connection."

"Alas, the revolutionaries rarely see the connection themselves until it is too late. If the problem with man is ignorance, then the solution is education. If the state can only provide free, mandatory education for all citizens, then utopia can become a reality. The only problem is that the social engineers who come to power invariably discover that there are certain people who are so corrupted that they cannot be reeducated—they can only be killed. Those people might be defined by their ethnicity, their religion, their class, or their profession, but however they are defined, they inevitably end up being purged from the body politic as if they were a cancer. Thus, Hitler massacred the Jews, Stalin the middle-class landowners, and Mao the intellectuals."

"Dad," said Stacey, who had also heard me lecture on this tragic topic, "tell them the quote from Solzhenitsyn."

"Thanks for reminding me, Stacey. Aleksandr Solzhenitsyn, who spent many long years in a Soviet prison and reeducation camp, eventually came to understand that the modern world has convinced itself of something that simply isn't true. Both sides in the Cold War firmly believed that the dividing line between good and evil runs between certain nations or parties or ideologies. But it does not."

"Then where does it run?" asked Sita.

"Right through the heart of every individual human being. How simple it would be if all the evil in the world were caused by one small group of bankers or Zionists or Freemasons. Then the solution would appear to be to jail or eliminate them. Well, throughout history this atrocious strategy has been tried again and again, with the same devastating results—creating not utopia but greater evil and suffering. No, the sin does not lie in groups but in each one of us.

"G. K. Chesterton once quipped that the biblical teaching of the fall of man is the only Christian doctrine that does not need to be proven. Just open your eyes and look around; evidence for the fall is everywhere. Something inside us is broken, and all the education and enlightenment in the world cannot fix it. One might as well try to cure a brain tumor with a handful of aspirins. No, the problem is serious; it calls for radical surgery."

"What surgery can eliminate sin?"

"That is the real question, Sita, the question that religions, including the Christian religion, avoid answering. Rather than face directly the central fact that willful sin has cut us off from our Creator—not to mention from others and from ourselves—religion tells us to keep trying harder. For all their appealing mysticism and search for enlightenment, Hinduism and Buddhism come down to karma, to winning favor with the creator—whether that is God or gods or the universe—by performing certain actions and avoiding other ones. Yes, Hindus and Buddhists give us many lives to accomplish that work while Jews, Christians, and Muslims give us only one, but all believe that, in some way or another, we must work for our salvation."

"Wait a minute," said Sita, "are you saying that Christianity is like all the other religions?"

"When it acts like a religion and nothing more, then it is not that different from Hinduism, Buddhism, Judaism, or Islam. There are many who grow up in Christian homes who, though they know we are sinners, still think they can earn salvation by good works. But that is not the message of Christ, the Bible, and the creeds of the church."

"What is that message?"

"That message, what Christians call the good news or gospel, is that we cannot of our own power remove from ourselves the sin that separates us from God. Such radical surgery can be accomplished only by God himself. That is why God came into the world and became one of us. Jesus, the second Adam, lived a sinless life of perfect obedience to God the Father. As such, he should have died peacefully and returned to God. Instead, he freely chose to take on himself the full weight of and punishment for our sins. When he died on the cross, sin died with him, but he did not stay in the grave. When he rose again from the dead, he overthrew the power of Satan, sin, and death, releasing a new, indestructible kind of life that he would share with all who would put their faith in him."

"That certainly sounds like good news," said Sita.

"I believe it is," I replied, "but only to someone who has first recognized the full problem of sin. Only once we accept the bad news, that we cannot deal with sin on our own, will we reach out and embrace the good news."

"Dr. Markos," said Anthony, who had been quietly working his way through his dinner plate, "I agree that this is good news, but there is something you said earlier that puzzles me."

"What's that?"

"You said that for Christians, the sins of the soul are far worse than the sins of the flesh? Is that right?"

"Yes. That is the reason the legalistic Pharisees rejected Jesus while the tax collectors and prostitutes followed him."

"But if that is the case, then why are Christians so obsessed with sex? Christians, at least in America, seem to treat sexual sins as the worst sins of all."

While Anthony was asking his questions, I had been in the process of securing a third helping of turkey and potatoes. The food never reached my mouth.

6

WHY ARE CHRISTIANS SO OBSESSED WITH SEX?

I COULD TELL THAT Anthony's question was a sincere one and that he was not trying to shock me or trap me. I also knew that he was not trying to justify himself, since he was a clean-living man of high moral character. Had he asked his question earlier, I might have tried to sneak my way out of addressing it, but, by this point in the dinner, all the guests were warm and well-fed, and a strong sense of openness and camaraderie filled the air.

"Anthony," I said, "your question is a fair one that really needs to be addressed. We live in a highly sexualized age when sex is used to sell everything from perfume to cars, food to clothing, medicine to smartphones. Since the 1960s, sex has been promoted as the most important thing in life, the thing that gives life joy and meaning and purpose. Movies, television, and magazines have all reinforced this glorification of sex until most people in our country, whatever their religion or lack of religion, believe it to be at the absolute center of a well-lived life. Indeed, most now believe that sex is an overwhelming force that cannot and should not be resisted. Have you noticed this?"

"Yes," said Anthony, "I have."

I could tell by the look in everyone else's eyes that they had as well.

"As a medical student, Anthony, you are well aware that man is in one sense part of the animal kingdom. Our bodies and their physical functions are very much like those of the higher mammals. Like them, we possess a strong biochemical urge to have sex and to procreate. You might even say that both humans and animals go into heat."

"You might say that," said Anthony with a smile.

"But what's the difference?"

"When animals go into heat, they are taken over and cannot help but seek a mate. When humans go into heat, they can resist the urge."

"In other words, we can choose whether to succumb to the physical urges that seize control of our bodies."

"Yes, I think that's a fair statement. Even doctors who do not believe in the soul realize that there is a part of us that stands outside nature and that chooses what stimuli to follow or not to follow."

"Alex," I said, "do you remember when we watched *The African Queen* together a few years back?"

"Yes," he said, "it was a great movie."

"Do you remember what Katherine Hepburn said to Humphrey Bogart when he said his alcoholism was just part of human nature?"

"I do! She said human nature was what we were put on this earth to rise above."

"Excellent! Though Hepburn's puritanical character overstates her case, there is much truth in the challenge she lays down to Bogart's boozy character. When we simply give in to our urges, we really are no better than animals. As humans, we have been gifted with consciousness, conscience, and free will. We are no more the slaves of our culture than we are of our biology. Yes, we are influenced by those things, sometimes strongly influenced, but there is a part of us that can rise above our culture and biology. Even when our body is literally enslaved to a master or a prison guard, our minds and souls remain free to think and wonder and dream."

"What about people who are mentally ill?" asked Anthony.

"Mental illness is actually one of those exceptions that proves the rule. If it can be shown in court that a murderer acted in a state of insane rage during which his rational capacities were overwhelmed, he will be sentenced to an inpatient psychiatric facility rather than a prison. But such sentences are rare. Ninety-nine percent of the time we are rational, moral agents, and the law treats us as such when we commit a crime."

"That's true. The law takes for granted that we choose our actions."

"Now imagine this scenario. A man rapes a woman and stands trial for it. If the prosecutor were to ask him why he committed the rape, and he were to answer that he couldn't help it because the woman's beauty triggered his sexual drive, would anyone in the courthouse accept that rationale?"

"I certainly wouldn't."

"Neither would anyone else. Even the greatest proponent of the sexual revolution would not accept it, for we all know that the choice of whether to have sex with someone is in fact a choice. We are the masters of our sexual drive, not vice versa. Yes, there are some rapists in psychiatric facilities, but again, that is the exception that proves the rule."

"But what about when the sex is consensual? I hope you are not arguing that all sex is criminal," said Anthony with a worried expression.

"No, no," I laughed, "not at all. So far, I have only been trying to establish that our sexual behavior is something we choose."

"But isn't that obvious?"

"Not anymore. A growing number of people today seem to think that if something is natural, it must be good. If I am a man and my natural urges draw me to want to have sex with a woman or a man, or many women or many men, the fact that I feel a strong physical desire in that direction does not make my acting on that desire a good or right or virtuous thing. A natural urge cannot be used to justify an illegal or immoral action.

"You need to explain that further."

"Anthony, have you ever heard of M. Scott Peck?"

"I think so. Wasn't he a psychiatrist?"

"Yes, he wrote a number of fine books, particularly *The Road Less Traveled* and *The People of the Lie*. In the former book, he reminds his readers that it is fully natural for babies to fill up their diapers."

"Dad," said Stacey, "is this really appropriate dinner conversation?"

"I suppose not," I said with an embarrassed smile, "but the matter is too important not to address it. In fact, I need to find the actual quote."

With that, I leaped from my chair and ran over to my bookshelf to find my copy of *The Road Less Traveled*. I went fast to make sure my daughter didn't have time to stop me.

When the book was securely in my hand and I had located the offending passage, I sat back down in my chair.

"All right, so that none of you will think that I was making up my last remark, I would like to read for you the whole passage. Although Peck calls on his readers to dedicate themselves to the pursuit of truth, he knows that many will refuse the challenge. He then goes on to explain:

> The tendency to avoid challenge is so omnipresent in human beings that it can properly be considered a characteristic of human nature. But calling it natural does not mean it is essential or beneficial or unchangeable behavior. It is also natural to defecate in our pants and never brush our teeth. Yet we teach ourselves to do the unnatural until the unnatural becomes itself second nature. Indeed, all self-discipline might be defined as teaching ourselves to do the unnatural. Another characteristic of human nature—perhaps the one that makes us most human—is our capacity to do the unnatural, to transcend and hence transform our own nature.

"Wow!" said Anthony. "Was Peck a Christian author?"

"That's an interesting question. When he wrote the words I just read, he was an open-minded seeker with an equal interest in Christianity and Zen Buddhism. By the time he finished his journey along the road less traveled, however, he had become a believer in Christ. Still, it was his experience as a psychotherapist rather than his later conversion that opened his eyes to the truth about human nature."

"It sounds like he would agree with that quote from Katherine Hepburn."

"He would, not because he was some kind of puritanical writer who wanted to spoil everyone's fun but because he knew that human beings are capable of so much more than animal existence. To truly grow as people, we must do things that go against our natural human desires: saying no to our sexual urges, or helping a person in need when we are busy and exhausted, or using the toilet instead of filling our diaper."

"Dad!"

"Sorry, Stacey, but we must all come to grips with the fact that not all desires are good ones. In many cases, we need to retrain our natural desires, to keep working on them until what at first seemed unnatural to us becomes second nature. That holds in particular for our sexual desires, which, if we did not train and discipline them, would impel us to sleep around before marriage and to be unfaithful after."

"But I thought," said Bill, who had been listening intently to the conversation, "that the church taught that sex is original sin."

When Bill asked his question, the room fell silent, and I took advantage of the silence to quickly compose my reply.

"Thanks so much, Bill," I said, when the hush had lifted from the table, "for having the courage to raise that issue. To be honest, before I really started studying Christianity and the Bible, I too thought that the church equated sex with original sin."

"Doesn't it?"

"No, it never did, and it never has. Oh, there have been individual believers and even some teachers who have taken that position, but even Augustine, who fashioned the doctrine of original sin as we know it and who chose for himself a celibate lifestyle, did not write or teach that. We fell through disobedience, not through sexual desire. Of course, in our fallen state, our sexual desires very often go awry and lead us into sin. But sex was neither a result nor a creation of the fall."

"Are you sure about that?"

"I am, and so were the church fathers. The matter is made clear in Genesis 2. God's command to Adam and Eve to be fruitful and multiply comes before our first parents ate of the fruit of the knowledge of good and evil and fell into sin. Indeed, marriage, and the sexual act that is central to it, is the only institution that predates the fall. While we were yet in Eden, marriage was divinely instituted with these words: 'Therefore a man shall leave his father and his mother and hold fast to his wife, and they shall become one flesh' (Gen 2:24)."

"Then why do so many Christians act as if sex were dirty and shameful?"

"Because, as we discussed earlier, many American Christians are dualists without knowing it. They've bought in to the Gnostic idea that flesh and matter are inherently evil and that we should therefore fix all our attention on the soul."

"Wait a minute," said Anthony, "when I was in your class, we read the *Confessions* of Saint Augustine. If I remember correctly, when Augustine was in his Gnostic phase, he was also living a life of sexual license."

"You remember well! There were Gnostic sects that would indulge in orgiastic behavior. But they did so, oddly enough, for the same reason many other Gnostic groups practiced strict celibacy."

"How could the same belief prompt such different behavior?"

"Because both the licentious Gnostics and the extreme ascetic ones shared a low view of the body that convinced them that the flesh had no ultimate value. Some ascetics rejected sex lest they have babies and thus increase the amount of bad flesh in the world. Others overindulged the flesh since the body was disposable and unimportant; it really made no difference what we did with it."

"But there aren't any Gnostic groups today, are they?"

"Not that I know of, but there *are* a significant number of married Christian couples today who, although they have sex and enjoy it, feel ashamed for doing so."

"Really?"

"If you think about my daughter's very American reaction to the passage I quoted from Peck, you will realize that there are two things that make Americans uncomfortable: sex and the bathroom."

"Wait a minute," David chimed in, "that reminds me of what you taught us in the other film class I took with you!"

"You remember well! In the Alfred Hitchcock class, we watched *Psycho*."

"I wish you had never shown me that film, Dad," said Stacey. "I think about it every time I take a shower!"

"It is a powerful film! In it, Hitch purposely plays on our double discomfort with sex and the bathroom. Shortly before our heroine is killed in the shower, we see her flush a piece of paper down a toilet. That was the first time in American cinema that a toilet was shown on the screen!"

"But what do sex and the bathroom have in common?" asked Anthony, whose logical, med-school mind was getting impatient with our tangent.

"They both have to do with the physical body, with our animal nature. They are reminders that we are not pure spirits like the angels but are embodied creatures who have to have sex to procreate and who have to go to the bathroom."

"Dad, do I have to remind you again that we are having dinner?"

"No, no, Stacey, this topic is too important to let it be disrupted by American squeamishness about natural physical functions. Alex, do you remember when we were waiting on line at the Miller Outdoor Theater concession stand and there was a man from Germany in front of us?"

"A man from Germany . . ."

"Yes, he wanted to know where the bathroom was, but because he was from Europe, he asked the lady at the counter if she could direct him to the nearest toilet."

"Oh yes," said Alex, "I remember now. When he used the word *toilet*, the lady got very upset and red in the face. After he left, we both heard her mumbling under her breath about how rude the man was."

"Exactly. The incident reminded me of one of my favorite C. S. Lewis stories. Toward the end of his life, Lewis was assisted by a young American secretary named Walter Hooper. Well, Hooper and Lewis were speaking on the first floor of Lewis's Oxford home one evening when Hooper asked Lewis whether he could use his bathroom. Without saying a word, Lewis led Hooper upstairs to a room with a bath in it, laid a towel over the edge of the tub, and silently returned downstairs.

"Several minutes later, a very sheepish-looking Hooper walked slowly back down the stairs. As he entered the study, Lewis looked up and said: 'That will teach you to abandon your silly American euphemisms. If you want the toilet, ask for it!'"

"That's a great story, Dad," said Alex. "What do you think, Stacey?"

"Hmmm!" was her only reply.

"It's a great story that highlights our American discomfort with the fleshiness of our bodies. Just as many northern Europeans have convinced themselves, falsely, that there is an essential link between cleanliness and godliness—most of the greatest saints of the Middle Ages were filthy—so many Americans have confused prudishness about the body with religious piety."

"But doesn't the Bible say that sex is bad?" said Bill, who had been patiently waiting to get the conversation back on track.

"It doesn't. We only *think* it does because of our American hangup with the body. It is quite true that the Bible forbids sex outside marriage, but that is because the Bible has a *high* view of sexuality."

"How can a religion that says you can only have sex with one person, and that that person must be your spouse, have a high view of sex?"

"Because Christianity teaches that sex is so special, so sacred, that it must be confined within the intimate, loving precincts of marriage."

"I'm not convinced."

"Let me try to explain it with an analogy. Stacey, what can you tell us about the plates we are using for dinner today?"

"We're using our finest china plates."

"Tell us, Stacey, do we use these plates every day? Do we use them to eat pizza or sandwiches or spaghetti?"

"No, we only use them a few times a year, usually Thanksgiving and Christmas."

"Why do we do that? Are we ashamed of them? Do we not want people to see them? It seems a bit of a waste to have such nice plates and only use them twice a year."

"Quite the opposite: It's because they are so precious that we only take them out for special occasions."

"Thank you, Stacey, you put that well. Bill, sex is like the fine chinaware we are eating from today. Sex must be confined to marriage, not because it is something dirty or bestial that we should be ashamed of but because it is good and beautiful and holy."

"That's an interesting analogy," said Bill.

"You see, it was not Christianity that robbed sexuality of its specialness and its sacredness but the sexual revolution of the 1960s and '70s. Since that time, sex has been reduced to nothing more than a physical urge. When people make love at the drop of a hat, the sexual act becomes as common and demystified as a handshake. Don't forget that without its pretty wings, a butterfly is nothing but an ugly black bug.

"Whenever I teach movies from the 1930s and '40s, I have to remind my students that the meaning of the phrase 'making love' shifted after the sexual revolution. Today, 'to make love' means simply to have sex. In older movies and songs, however, it carried the fuller connotation of romancing a lady, of wooing her with words and gestures."

"I see your point, but aren't you exaggerating when you say that the Bible treats sexuality as sacred? Isn't sex presented solely as the means of procreation?"

"It isn't in the Song of Solomon. That beautiful book from the Old Testament celebrates love in all its fullness: emotional, spiritual, and sexual. But it also warns three times not to 'stir up or awaken love until it pleases' (Song 2:7; 3:5; 8:4). The Song treats love and sex as powerful things that must never be trifled with. In the climax of the poem, we are assured that 'love is strong as death,' that it is like a raging fire that 'many waters cannot quench,' that 'if a man offered for love, all the wealth of his house,' he 'would be utterly despised' (Song 8:6-7)."

"But isn't that just poetic exaggeration?"

"It is in part, but it is supported by one of the most surprising verses in the Old Testament. In Deuteronomy, this law is recorded: 'When a man is newly married, he shall not go out with the army or be liable for any other public duty. He shall be free at home one year to be happy with his wife whom he has taken' (Deut 24:5). The implication of this verse in Hebrew is that the soldier will please his wife sexually."

"That sounds like a good idea to me," said Bill, "but I don't see how it suggests that sex is somehow sacred."

"Ah, for that we must turn to a verse in the New Testament that explains the deeper spiritual mystery that lurks behind human sexuality. In his epistle to the church at Ephesus, Paul, in the midst of a discussion about husbands and wives, reiterates the Bible's original definition of marriage: 'Therefore a man shall leave his father and mother and hold fast to his wife, and the two shall become one flesh' (Eph 5:31). But he does not stop there. Having defined marriage and sexuality as that which makes the two into one, Paul explains that the marital-sexual union of man and wife points forward to a greater union: 'This mystery is profound, and I am saying that it refers to Christ and the church' (Eph 5:32).

"According to Paul, sexual union is in part a foreshadowing of heaven, when Christ will be united to his bride, the church, and the two shall be one. That is to say, we will be united with Christ while continuing to remain ourselves. Every marriage and every sexual union speaks in advance of that greatest of mysteries by which we can be one with God in heaven without losing our own integrity as a unique individual self created in the image of God."

"That is all quite beautiful," said Bill, "but I still don't see why the church is so hung up about strictly confining sex to a husband and wife."

"I know it may sound strange to our modern, scientific ears, but, from the point of view of God, when a man and a woman have sex, they truly do become one flesh. Sex is not just a physical act; it has a metaphysical dimension as well that transcends the natural, material world. It is never *just* sex; the union goes much deeper than that."

"Does the Bible really say that, or are we just reading that into it?"

"Actually, there is a passage about sexual immorality in Paul's first letter to the church at Corinth that states it in very bold language. The Corinthians were notorious for being lax in their sexual practices, so Paul had to make his case quite strongly if he was to convince them that God meant for sex to be confined to marriage. Shall I read it?"

"Please do."

> The body is not meant for sexual immorality, but for the Lord, and the Lord for the body. And God raised the Lord and will also raise us up by his power. Do you not know that your bodies are members of Christ? Shall I then take the members of Christ and make them members of a prostitute? Never! Or do you not know that he who is joined to a prostitute becomes one body with her? For, as it is written, "The two will become one flesh." But he who is joined to the Lord becomes one spirit with him. Flee from sexual immorality. Every other sin a person commits is outside the body, but the sexually immoral person sins against his own body. Or do you not know that your body is a temple of the

> Holy Spirit within you, whom you have from God? You are not your own, for you were bought with a price. So glorify God in your body. (1 Cor 6:13-20)

"I must admit that Paul's language is quite strong."

"It is, not because Paul is being legalistic or overly critical but because he is drawing out the full implications of many of the things we have been discussing today. Please notice that the passage begins by affirming the bodily resurrection of Christ. The very fact that God took on human flesh and then maintained that flesh after death affirms the high value God places on the body. Sexual immorality is bad because it violates the sanctity of the body. If the body were unimportant, as it was for the Gnostics, then sexual immorality would not be a big deal. But it *is* a big deal, because God highly values and honors the flesh that he both created and assumed."

"I notice that in the passage you read, Paul quotes again that verse from Genesis about the two becoming one flesh."

"Good point. Everything Christianity has to say about marriage and sexuality goes back to that key verse. As we said earlier, if we don't know the purpose for which something was made, we will run the risk of breaking or even destroying it. God himself defines marriage as the two into one, but that is also how he defines the relationship between the believer and Christ. That is why, in the previous passage I read, Paul links human marriage and sexuality to the coming great marriage of Christ and the church."

"But what does Paul mean by calling our body the temple of the Holy Spirit?"

"In the Old Testament, the Spirit of God rested on the ark of the covenant, which was kept in the holy of holies, the innermost part of the temple in Jerusalem. That temple was destroyed by the Romans in AD 70 and has never been rebuilt. But that was not a problem for the Jews who accepted Christ. According to the New Testament, when a believer accepts Christ as his savior, the Holy Spirit comes and dwells within him. That is to say, each individual believer is now the temple, the very place where the Spirit of God dwells."

"That's a pretty shocking claim."

"It is, one that is sure to ruffle a few modernist feathers. But Paul says something else that is even more guaranteed to confuse and anger the modern man. He says very clearly that our bodies are not our own but were bought by the blood Christ shed on the cross. Or to put it another way, we do not own our bodies."

"That may be the most shocking thing you've said today."

"You are right. Most Americans, even many who call themselves evangelical Christians, take for granted that they own their own bodies. That is why the four major cultural changes that came out of the sexual revolution all rest on the belief that we own our bodies and can therefore decide for ourselves what to do with them."

"What four things?"

"The first is the relaxing, if not the elimination, of the traditional stricture that sex is to be confined to marriage. The second is no-fault divorce, which says we can break from our spouse without giving any just cause if we feel unhappy or unfulfilled. The third is abortion on demand, with its stigmatizing of anyone who would tell a woman what she can do with her body. The fourth is the gay-rights movement that has climaxed today with the legalization of gay marriage. Though these four issues are all distinctive, they all take for granted the presupposition that our bodies are our own to do with as we see fit."

"Hey Dad," said Stacey, "it sounds to me like you are getting political. What do you say we move back to the den and sing some songs?"

"Stacey, my daughter, thank you for that helpful bit of feminine advice! We can't tackle religion *and* politics in the same evening! Let us indeed move back into the den for some music."

THIRD COURSE

DESSERT BY CANDLELIGHT

7

WHY WOULD A JUST GOD CHOOSE A SINGLE NATION?

I AM CONTINUALLY THANKFUL that the man from whom I took piano lessons when I was a boy taught me how to improvise. Because of his instruction, I can play almost any song the first time I see it as long as I have the melody line and the chords. Better yet, once I learned how to improvise a song on the piano using only the melody and chords to guide me, I was able to purchase a series of fake books that, under a single cover, provide the melody, chords, and lyrics for hundreds of songs. Thus, while my Disney and Christmas fake books include 200 and 275 songs, respectively, my Broadway and movie fake books weigh in at 720 and 450 songs each.

But best of all for someone like me who has led student and international Bible study groups in his home for the past three decades is the hymn fake book, which crams into one, single, glorious, spiral-bound paperback over one thousand hymns from every possible denomination! With that book on my piano, I can honor almost any request, though we usually confine ourselves to the hundred-plus hymns and chorus songs whose lyrics appear on my twenty-page homemade song sheets.

Once our well-fed bodies were settled back into the den, I began the singing with the traditional Thanksgiving hymn, "We Gather Together." After that, I opened the floor to suggestions. For the next thirty minutes we moved joyously from "Be Thou My Vision" to "It Is Well with My Soul" to "Amazing Grace" to "What Wondrous Love Is This" to "This Is My Father's

World" to "Nearer My God to Thee" to "Rock of Ages" to "Come Thou Fount of Every Blessing."

When we finished the last song, I turned on the piano bench to solicit one more suggestion, but before I could do that, Anthony broke in: "Dr. Markos, I'm sorry to interrupt the singing again, but do you mind if I ask a question about the song we just sang?"

"Please do," I replied.

"It has to do with the opening line of the second verse: 'Here I raise mine Ebenezer.' Can somebody please tell me what an Ebenezer is? The only Ebenezer I've heard of is Ebenezer Scrooge!"

"I'm glad you had the courage to ask that question, Anthony. My guess is that most people who sing that song in church have no idea what an Ebenezer is. Heck, I only know myself because I looked it up in a Bible encyclopedia several years back!"

"What does it mean?"

"In 1 Samuel, the great prophet-judge Samuel prayed to the Lord that he would rescue the people of Israel from the Philistines who had been oppressing them for many years. In response, God sent a divine thunderstorm that terrified the Philistines and allowed the Israelites to slaughter them. To commemorate this deliverance from their longtime enemies, Samuel set up a stone and named it Ebenezer, which in Hebrew means 'stone of help' (1 Sam 7:10-12)."

"I never would have guessed that," said Anthony, "but it makes sense. When we sing in the song about raising our Ebenezer, we are thanking God for his help and protection."

"Exactly," I replied with a smile. "When Samuel set up his Ebenezer, he was following in the tradition of Joshua, who, each time he conquered one of the tribes of Canaan, set up a standing stone to memorialize the victory and God's deliverance."

"Just a minute," said Ali, who had been listening carefully to my exchange with Anthony. "You said many things at dinner that I found interesting, but I have a problem with what you just said."

"What do you mean?"

"You said that God helped the Jews to conquer and destroy the different nations who were living in Canaan at the time. Why would a just and loving God do that? Why would he favor one nation over other nations?"

"I see your point, Ali. To be honest, your question may be the hardest one that has been raised today. I would like us to discuss it at length, but first I must ask a favor."

"What is that?"

"Well, your question opens two possible paths of discussion: The first takes us back to the Old Testament; the second takes us forward to the modern state of Israel. Ali, I know you have some Palestinian friends who have suffered unfairly at the hands of the Israeli government. Still, I want to avoid taking us down the black hole of politics. We've already pushed the envelope speaking so much about religion; to try to tackle the Israeli question as well would be asking for trouble!"

I could tell that Ali, a passionate man of strong convictions who had traveled most of the globe and witnessed firsthand some of the major political upheavals of the twentieth century, wanted to debate the actions and policies of the Jewish state, but he graciously acquiesced to my request.

"All right," he said, "we can leave the politics of Palestine out, but you still have to address the deeper issue that lies beneath the claims of ancient and modern Israel alike. I mean the issue of the Jews being the chosen people. That's the part I don't accept. God would not choose one group or nation over another."

"Ali, you might be surprised to know that many modern Jews are equally uncomfortable with the idea of chosenness. In fact, they are positively embarrassed by it. They reject any claim to being specially chosen or set apart by God."

"Good for them!"

"Actually, one of the first philosophers to argue against the chosenness of the Jews was himself Jewish. Do you know who I'm referring to?"

"Of course! You mean Spinoza, one of the greatest philosophers in history. His own people persecuted him and threw him out of the synagogue."

"Baruch Spinoza was a man of great courage, and I'm glad, Ali, that you encouraged me to spend more time reading and studying his writing. He foresaw many of the advances in science and psychology that we take for granted today, and he stood bravely for religious tolerance. But I think Spinoza was profoundly mistaken about a central presupposition that he assumes but never proves."

"What presupposition is that?"

"That God is neither more nor less than the laws of nature. He is not a personal being who knows and can be known but an impersonal force of rationality that orders the cosmos. For Spinoza, God and nature are equally eternal."

"Wasn't he correct?"

"Not according to the discoveries of modern science. What we have learned from the Big Bang is that space, time, and matter all had a beginning. The universe was not always there; it came into being at a specific moment some fourteen billion years ago. But if there was a time when it came into being, then there must be something eternal that existed before the beginning of nature: for, as philosophers and scientists both know, nothing can come out of nothing."

"But if God created nature, then who created God?"

"No one created God, for God, unlike nature, is eternal. Spinoza dismissed the story of Moses and the burning bush as superstition, but it was at the burning bush that God revealed his true name: 'I am who I am' (Ex 3:14). God, as the philosophers would put it, is the only being whose existence and essence are one and the same. The universe, the angels, the beasts, and we ourselves all came into existence; God simply is."

"What does that have to do with the chosenness of the Jews?"

"If God is not merely a force or an energy or a set of abstract laws, if he is, as the Bible claims, a person, then it should not shock us that God, as a person, likes some things and dislikes others. One of the qualities of persons is that they choose."

"Spinoza would call that an example of anthropomorphism: of the writers of the Bible making God in their own image."

"It is true that whenever we write or think about God, there is a danger we will project our own likes and dislikes onto him. But there is an equal and opposite danger, one that Spinoza himself falls into. That's the danger of saying that if we are personal, God must be impersonal."

"What's wrong with saying that?"

"Because God is not less than us; he is more than us. Aristotle explains it this way. Plants are alive and grow. Animals, which belong to a higher category than plants, share with those plants the qualities of life and growth. But to those qualities they add the ability to move. Humans, like the plants and animals beneath them, live and grow and move, but they also think and reason. As you move up the scale of being, things get richer and more complex. God is not a man who has had his personality effaced; he is more than man and thus more than personal. He is, if you will, transpersonal. Our personality is an echo of the fuller, more perfect personality of our Creator."

"Perhaps, but if God really is fuller and more perfect than we are, wouldn't he treat and love all nations the same?"

"Yes, but with two caveats. First, treating all nations the same carries with it the stipulation that all nations be held to the same standard. If a nation violates that standard, and God destroys it, that does not mean he is playing favorites. Second, the fact that God loves all nations and peoples equally does not mean that God cannot choose one nation as the vehicle through which to show his love to all the other nations."

"But the writers of the Old Testament claim that God chose to bless only Israel."

"Not exactly. When God called Abraham out of Ur and sent him to the land of Canaan, he *did* promise that he would make him into a great nation and that he would bless those who blessed him and curse those who cursed him. He *did* choose Abraham and his descendants, and he *did* give them a privileged place and calling. But he did so for a reason that was much larger than Abraham and the Jewish people."

"What reason could justify God singling out one people to be his chosen race?"

"Here's what God said to Abraham: 'Go from your country and your kindred and your father's house to the land that I will show you. And I will make of you a great nation, and I will bless you and make your name great, so that you will be a blessing. I will bless those who bless you, and him who dishonors you I will curse, and in you all the families of the earth shall be blessed' (Gen 12:1-3). Do you see how God blessed Abraham so that he could be a blessing to all the other nations?"

"But did the Jews follow that calling?"

"Well, to be honest, they very often shirked their duty. But when they shirked it, God punished them as harshly, and often more harshly, than he did the other nations."

"I don't like all this talk about punishing and killing. Isn't God a God of love?"

"Dr. Markos," said David, who had been listening quite intently and could see that I was unsure of how to address Ali's question, "don't you think it would be a good idea to go back to the beginning and explain God's wider plan?"

"Thanks, David, that's an excellent suggestion. It usually is a good idea to begin at the beginning!"

With that, I leapt off the piano bench and moved to the center of the den. When I did that, the room fell silent, and all eyes turned to me. I took a deep breath and began . . .

"In the beginning," I said, unconsciously deepening my voice to sound like the narrator of an old Hollywood biblical epic, "God created the heavens and the earth. He shaped our planet and filled it with life and, when he was done, he crowned his creation by making us in his own image.

"That does not mean," I continued, shifting from my movie voice to my professor voice, "that we look like God or that God has a body; it means that God gifted us with consciousness and reason and made us into moral agents who can choose, who can appreciate beauty, and who can know God. God gave us all we needed to grow and thrive, but we chose to disobey him and to go our own way."

"That's just superstition about gardens and apples and talking snakes."

"There again Spinoza would agree with you, but I don't want to focus now on the intersection between the historical and the mythic. Let's return instead to something we discussed during dinner. However literally you read the story of the fall in Genesis, the fact is that there is a problem with man, and as we said before, that problem is not ignorance but sin. We commit evil acts not because we are ignorant but because we are rebellious. We don't lack knowledge; we lack obedience. And that sin and disobedience can be seen in every human being, from the most innocent seven-year-old boy to the sincerest preacher to the sweetest grandmother.

"The story of the Bible is, in great part, the story of God dealing with sin and its terrible consequences. Ultimately, God would break the power of sin through the death and resurrection of his son, but that world-changing event would come at the climax of a long historical process. Did you know that God prophesied and promised that event and that climax immediately after the fall of Adam and Eve?"

"How?"

"After cursing the snake to drag its belly in the dust, God made this prophetic promise: 'I will put enmity between you and the woman, and between your offspring and her offspring; he shall bruise your head, and you shall bruise his heel' (Gen 3:15). The seed of the serpent is Satan, the fallen angel who accuses us ceaselessly before God; the seed of the woman will, in the fullness of time, be the Messiah. The devil bruised the heel of Christ when he convinced the Jews and Romans to crucify him, but that very victory led to Christ crushing the head of Satan when he rose from the dead."

"That's impressive, but what does it have to do with God choosing the Jews?"

"God did at first try to work with the full population of the world, but that proved impossible. The wickedness and rebelliousness of man was so great that it led to the flood and the Tower of Babel."

"More killing."

"Ali, like you, I find it hard to take in the full scale of God's wrath, but that is because we are both men of the modern world and, as such, have lost our reverence for the holiness of God and our outrage at the depravity to which we are capable. And we must remember that God provided a way out in the form of the ark. Noah and his family availed themselves of that means of escape, but the rest of the world rejected it."

"Were the Jews any better than anyone else?"

"Not necessarily, though their founder, Abraham, won God's favor by placing his full faith in the promises of God (Gen 15:4-6). After the flood and Babel, God chose to narrow his focus to a single nation, for through that nation he would preserve the bloodline of the promised deliverer who would crush the head of Satan. That sacred bloodline would pass down from Abraham to Isaac to Jacob to Judah. From Judah it would pass down to King David, and from David it would pass down to Jesus. But that was not the only reason God zeroed in on the Jews."

"What was the other reason?"

"Through the Jews, God brought his sacred law into the world. The reason the people of the other nations continually gave way to sin and depravity was that they abandoned the true God to worship idols. God separated the Jews from the other nations so that they would remain pure and would worship God alone."

"Did they remain pure?"

"Alas, most turned to idolatry, but within Israel God always preserved a faithful remnant who worshiped him and him alone (1 Kings 19:15-18). Most modern people get uncomfortable when they read in the Bible that God is a jealous God, but they forget that God literally took Israel as his bride. When the Jews turned from God to worship idols, they were literally committing adultery."

"Jealousy does not seem like an appropriate emotion for God."

"What would you think of a man who, when his wife announced to him, without any sense of shame or remorse, that she was sleeping with other men, shrugged his shoulders and said that it was no big deal? A husband who reacted that way would not be a husband who loved his wife or took seriously their marriage vow. There are times when jealousy is the only right and proper response. God did not see it as no big deal when his bride fornicated with the pagan nations. He felt the same way Jesus felt when he went into the holy temple of Jerusalem and found moneychangers fleecing the faithful for their own dishonest gain. He didn't say it was no big deal; he overturned their tables and then chased them out with a whip."

"I rather like that part."

"So do I, but that's because we all know there is a right and proper time for jealousy and righteous anger. When something sacred and holy has been violated, the only correct response is a burning zeal for purity. That is why Americans, despite having accepted pornography, are still enraged at child pornography—even the sexual revolution has not stamped out our sense of outrage when the innocence of children is sullied."

"I can understand why God would want to keep the Jews separate and holy from the other nations, but why did he give them land that belonged to others? Is God a thief who steals land away to give to his favorites?"

"Ali, I can't tell you precisely why God wanted the Jews to live in the land of Canaan, but I can tell you something that is often overlooked by readers of the Bible. If you recall the story of Abraham, you will remember that God called Abraham to forsake his home country for the land of promise, the land flowing with milk and honey. And yet, despite that promise, the Jews did not actually acquire that land for some four hundred years. Abraham, Isaac, and Jacob all lived as strangers in a strange land. Jacob's son Joseph led the Jews into Egypt, where they endured bitter centuries of slavery until Moses led them out of Egypt into the Promised Land. Why the delay?"

"I'm not sure. You'll have to answer that one."

"Luckily, that is a question I *can* answer because God explains it clearly to Abraham. Here is what he says:

> Know for certain that your offspring will be sojourners in a land that is not theirs and will be servants there, and they will be afflicted for four hundred years. But I will bring judgment on the nation that they serve, and afterward they shall come out with great possessions. As for you, you shall go to your fathers in peace; you shall be buried in a good old age. And they shall come back here in the fourth generation, for the iniquity of the Amorites is not yet complete. (Gen 15:13-16)

"What God is telling Abraham here is that he will not yet give him the Promised Land, for there are people living in it who have not reached the level of depravity that led to the flood and Babel. Only once the nations of Canaan had become thoroughly wicked did God displace them and give their land to the Israelites."

"What kind of wickedness could justify that?"

"Archaeologists have excavated the ruins of the nations of Canaan, and they have learned that the people there were wicked in at least two ways. Their idolatrous religion led them into a kind of sexual depravity that equated human fornication with natural fertility. They prostituted their own daughters in service to evil deities. Worse yet, in order to win the favor of gods such as Moloch and Baal, they sacrificed their own children: passing them through the fire to appease their vengeful gods (Jer 7:31). In fact, one of the words used for 'hell' in the New Testament, *Gehenna*, comes from the valley where those innocent children were brutally sacrificed."

"How do we know the Jews weren't just using that as an excuse to plunder the goods of the Canaanites?"

"Because when the Jews defeated the Canaanites, God ordered them to destroy everything. They were not to profit from wealth linked to such idolatry. Yes, they did win the land itself, but they were to destroy everything else. There were some Jews who kept the spoils for themselves, but when they did so, God punished them (Josh 7)."

"I thought God is supposed to be a forgiving God."

"God did show mercy to some Canaanites who recognized both the wickedness of their civilization and the special calling of the Jews. When Joshua sent men to spy out the city of Jericho before attacking it, the spies were helped by a woman named Rahab, who was, believe it or not, a prostitute. Though she was herself a sinner, she recognized that God was working through the Jews. Because of this she and her family were spared when God tore down the walls of Jericho."

"What about the other citizens of Jericho?"

"Listen to what Rahab says to the spies when she encounters them:

> I know that the Lord has given you the land, and that the fear of you has fallen upon us, and that all the inhabitants of the land melt away before you. For we have heard how the Lord dried up the water of the Red Sea before you when you came out of Egypt, and what you did to the two kings of the Amorites who were beyond the Jordan, to Sihon and Og, whom you devoted to destruction. And as soon as we heard it, our hearts melted, and there was no spirit left in

> any man because of you, for the Lord your God, he is God in the heavens above and on the earth beneath. (Josh 2:9-11)

"What point are you trying to make?"

"The point is that the people of Jericho knew full well that God was with the Jews, but they refused to heed the warning. It seems clear from the story that if others in Jericho had shown the faith and humility of Rahab, they too could have been spared. If enough had done so, they could have opened the gates and let the Jews in rather than have their walls divinely thrown down. But they did not, nor did the other nations of Canaan. In addition to the sacred prostitution and child sacrifice, they had turned themselves away from their Creator in rigid pride and disobedience."

"But does that really give the Jews the right to their land?"

"Actually, Ali, though the Jews were given the land, it was always given to them conditionally. When they turned to idolatry themselves and became as wicked as the Canaanites, God took the land away from them. First the Northern Kingdom of Israel, which had always been more wicked than the south, was destroyed by the Assyrians; then the Southern Kingdom of Judah, when it too fell into utter depravity, was destroyed and sent into exile by the pagan nation of Babylon.

"Ali, I know that many people today are offended by the idea of there being a chosen people, but we must never forget that being chosen does not mean having everything given to you on a silver platter. To be chosen is to be set apart, and that usually brings sacrifice and suffering."

"Hey, Dad," said Stacey, "tell Ali what Tevye says in *Fiddler on the Roof* about the Jews being the chosen people."

"Go ahead, Stacey! Tell us."

"I don't remember the exact words, but he says to God that although he knows it's an honor to be the chosen people, he wouldn't mind if God would choose someone else once in a while!"

"Exactly! I sometimes have Christian students tell me that they would like to be prophets. When they say that, I always remind them that all the prophets in the Bible suffered, and most of them were killed."

"But those prophets only cared about Israel, never about the other nations."

"Actually, most of the prophets issued warnings to the other nations as well, but they, like the men of Jericho, refused to listen. There was, however, one prophet who perfectly matches your description. God ordered him to go to Nineveh and preach the word of God to the Assyrians. But he refused to go, because the Assyrians were enemies of Israel, and the ethnocentric prophet did not want them to repent and be forgiven."

"What prophet was that?"

"He's a prophet everyone has heard of. His name was Jonah."

"You mean the one who was swallowed by the whale?"

"The same. When God called him to go to Nineveh, he sailed off in the opposite direction, thinking he could somehow outrun God's call. But God caught up with him and caused a storm until the pagan sailors were forced to toss Jonah overboard to save the ship. That's when the giant fish swallowed him and carried him to Nineveh. In the end, Jonah preached the message God sent him to deliver, and just as he feared, the Assyrians repented in sackcloth and ashes. Jonah was furious, and God had to work hard to convince Jonah that he cared about the cruel Assyrians and not only the Jews (Jon 4)."

"Are you saying that God reprimanded Jonah for not caring about Nineveh?"

"Yes. God forced Jonah to go, and when his message led the Ninevites to confess and seek God's pardon, God forgave them. Alas, Nineveh later returned to her wicked ways, but that wasn't God's fault. His desire was for the Assyrians to follow his path."

"I'm surprised the book of Jonah made it into the Bible!"

"I'll bet there were some who tried to remove it, but it's there, and it attests to God's love for all the nations. That love is also attested to in Matthew's genealogy of Christ (Mt 1:1-17). In it, he lists only four women from the Old Testament: Tamar, Rahab, Ruth, and Bathsheba. As far as we can tell, all four were Gentiles whom God graciously allowed not only into Israel but into the sacred bloodline of the Messiah.

"And one more thing. Just as God had to put Jonah through great adversity to teach him his duty and responsibility toward the Gentiles, so God had to do the same to the early Jewish Christians who wanted to keep the gospel for themselves in Jerusalem. God was forced to use persecution and ultimately the destruction of the temple by the Romans to convince the early Christians that they were to share the good news with the Gentiles and let them come into the church on equal footing. He even had to grab hold of an angry, rabidly ethnocentric Jewish Pharisee named Saul and convert him into Paul, the great missionary to the Gentiles. Heck, if it weren't for Paul, the early Jewish Christians would likely have forced Gentile converts to get circumcised!"

"Three cheers for Paul!"

"Indeed! Ali, I don't want to lessen the seriousness of the questions you have raised. I struggle myself with the killing in the Old Testament, as do all Christians, but those terrible events must be viewed in terms of God's overall plan of salvation. Though we certainly see more of God's wrath in the Old Testament and more of his mercy in the New, it is still the same God: a God of both justice and forgiveness, holiness and mercy.

"It is true that we all want a God of grace who forgives and shows mercy to all, but we also want to know that there is real justice in the universe: that true evil will be punished and defeated, and true goodness will win out in the end."

"I think that is something we can agree on! But I'm afraid I have another question that you have not yet addressed."

"What is that?"

"Why do Christians think that their religion is the only way to heaven?"

I opened my mouth to speak, but before a single word could come out, my daughter threw herself between me and the guests and waved her hands frantically.

"No, no, no! No more talking until we've had our dessert. There are five different pies and dozens of cookies on the dining room table that are waiting to be eaten."

Stacey didn't have to say another word. Ten seconds later, the den was empty.

8

HOW CAN THERE BE ONLY ONE WAY TO GOD?

THE PIES TASTED SO DELICIOUS they almost made me forget Ali had dropped another difficult question on my plate that I would soon have to take up. Still, I did my best to make my dessert linger by smothering my first piece of pie with two scoops of vanilla ice cream and my second with a generous dollop of whipped cream. As I reveled briefly in the sugar high produced by two pieces of pie topped by two varieties of cream, I racked my brain to find a way to begin my response.

"Ladies and gentlemen," I said, putting down my fork and running my napkin across my mouth, "Ali has asked a very important question about the relationship between Christianity and the other religions of the world. Let me begin my response by making a bold statement: Christianity is not the only truth!"

When I said those words, Alex, Stacey, and David looked at me as if I had lost my mind, while my guests who were either seekers or members of other religions looked shocked and a bit puzzled. Ali smiled as if to say, "Now you are talking sense!"

"I'm sure most of you weren't expecting me to say that," I continued, "but I will repeat what I just said: Christianity is not the only truth."

"Then why," asked Ali, "do Christians say that Jesus is the only way to God?"

"Because," I replied, "though Christianity is not the *only* truth, it is the only *complete* truth. We are all made in God's image, and we all possess a natural yearning for God. That is why enduring truths about God and man, morality and salvation, the universe and the afterlife can be found in the writings of all the great philosophers and holy men from Moses to Socrates, Confucius to Buddha, Zoroaster to Muhammad. We are as much *homo sapiens* (thinking man) as we are *homo religiosus* (religious man). Thinking about God and the soul and heaven is as natural and essential to us as thinking about food and shelter and clothing. But, I would argue, only in Christ do those scattered truths find their fullness and their completion."

"It is my belief," said Ali, "that all religion rises out of man's fear of death. I will never forget when my grandson first realized that he would die someday. With a sad expression in his eyes, he looked up at me and said, 'Grandpa, I don't want to die.'"

"That's a powerful story, Ali, and a universal one. But it raises the question of why the thought of our own demise should fill us with such horror and dismay. Why are we, as a species, so often paralyzed by what Hamlet calls 'the dread of something after death'? Men tremble and are frightened when they find themselves in a graveyard. But no animal feels terrified in the presence of dead animals. I'm inclined to think that our feelings of dread are a pointer to something beyond ourselves and our world."

"Not for Confucius and not for certain types of Chinese Buddhism. Confucius wisely realized that we could know nothing about heaven or hell or the afterlife and that we would therefore do better to keep our focus on this world. That's why the Chinese are the masters of food and of health, and why many of their greatest leaders organized their kingdoms around the secular principles laid down by Confucius. The Chinese seek balance in this world and the flourishing of human civilization and don't concern themselves much with the next."

"On the surface, that is very true. The Chinese do tend to keep their focus on this world. And yet, at the same time, the Chinese are strongly aware of a spiritual realm where the souls of their ancestors reside. And, of course, there are tens of millions of Buddhists who believe in reincarnation. Even the down-to-earth Chinese are haunted by a realm beyond our realm, a world that rises above ours as the mountains of Tibet rise above the great grasslands of central Asia. Even the most secular of their emperors sought to discern the mandate of heaven."

"If I may," said Elaine politely, "I have been listening to your conversation with great interest. Ali is right about Confucius and how his teachings are grounded in this world, but you are also right that the Chinese are a religious people who seek to imitate the Buddha and who are concerned about the afterlife. What I would like to know is why Christians do not accept reincarnation. Don't they believe the soul is immortal?"

"Yes, Christians do believe the soul is immortal, but they also believe that there is an incarnational relationship between our body and our soul. Our body is more than a temporary container for our soul; the two are intimately connected. We are not a soul trapped in a body but an enfleshed or embodied soul. Or, to put it another way, we are fully physical and fully spiritual, not half and half. That is why, as we discussed earlier, the Bible teaches that in heaven our redeemed soul will be reunited with our resurrected body so that we will continue to be an enfleshed soul for all eternity."

"I still don't understand why anyone would want to be trapped in a body for all eternity."

"Elaine, as you did before with your comment about the body and the soul, you have hit on the essential question. For the Stoic and Epicurean philosophers who lived at the time of Jesus, the Christian claim that Jesus rose bodily from the dead was nonsensical. For the Gnostics, it was the highest blasphemy. Why would a pure God link himself to fallen flesh and then keep that flesh for eternity? For them, freedom and salvation meant leaving the bodily and the material behind."

"As a Buddhist, I still think they're right. The body and its desires must be left behind to achieve true salvation."

As I pondered our last few minutes of discussion, I realized we were rehashing rather than developing the discussion we had had earlier. I needed to find another approach that would make clear the difference between salvation from sin and death and salvation from the body and its desires.

As I slowly shifted my gaze away from Elaine and toward the kitchen in search of inspiration, my eyes fell upon a candle in the window. As unobtrusively as I could, I slipped into the kitchen and took hold of the candle and a book of matches. I lit the candle and carried it back into the den.

"Elaine," I said, carefully handing her the lit candle, "can you please illustrate for the group the Buddhist concept of nirvana?"

"Certainly," she said. She held the candle before her face and, with one gentle puff of air, blew it out.

"Please explain," I said.

"Well," she said, "although we believe in reincarnation, we hope that a time will come when we will escape from the endless cycle of birth, death, and rebirth—what we call the wheel of samsara—and join with the universe. Then, our individual self, with all its pain and desire, will be extinguished like this candle."

"Thank you, Elaine, for explaining that. I have always held a respectful fascination for the Eastern yearning to achieve nirvana. Still, I would argue that the true Christian vision of heaven surpasses nirvana in an important way. Christ promises his disciples that in heaven they will achieve the redemption, purification, and perfection of their desires. Nirvana, in contrast, promises only the extinction of desire."

"Yes, that's correct."

"But in eliminating the pain and negative desires that come with selfhood, the pleasures and positive desires are also destroyed. Can it really be that all our desires and joys and hopes and dreams will end in extinction?"

"How else can we know true bliss without that extinction?"

"But what does bliss mean if the one who has yearned for it all his life no longer exists? Another way nirvana is described is as a vast ocean into which the drop of our selfhood is spilled and loses itself."

"But is that not a good thing?"

"Elaine, it may surprise you to know that there have been thinkers in the West, up to this day, who view heaven as one soul into which our individual soul is merged and loses itself. I must admit that there are days in my life when such an annihilation of the self, with all its endless anxieties and conflicting desires, seems, to quote Hamlet again, 'a consummation devoutly to be wished.' But can that really be the destiny of man?"

"But if we don't achieve nirvana, then we'll be trapped forever in the wheel."

"Yes, if reincarnation were true, then perhaps nirvana would provide the only means of escape from the futility of that wheel. But if reincarnation is true, then it means we don't really have a self that can be extinguished. As we move from one incarnation to the next, our selfhood is ultimately discarded along with our body. The laws of karma determine our next incarnation, but any sense of a real, integral 'I' gets lost as we move from one new form to the next. Can it really be that the multilife search for enlightenment should lead in the end to the extinction of the self who sought after it?"

"Louis," said Ali, who had been looking for a pause so he could get back into the conversation, "I think you are evading the question we started with?"

"How do you mean?"

"You haven't said yet why Christians think their religion is the only way to God."

"Thanks for getting us back on track, Ali, though we haven't strayed as far away from that initial question as it may seem. The real issue is not whether the Christian or the Buddhist is the better person, or even whether Christianity or Buddhism offers the best code for living one's life. The real question is, What does it mean to get to God, to go to heaven, to be saved?"

"Isn't that obvious?"

"Not if you think about what Elaine just said. For a Christian, heaven means achieving salvation *of* the self; for Buddhism, nirvana means salvation *from* the self. The former promises joy perfected, the latter an end to sorrow and joy alike. As strange as it may seem, the final goal of Buddhism, and Hinduism as well, is not that different from the final goal of atheism."

"How can you say that?"

"I once asked an atheist how he could go on living if he believed that when he died, he would be buried and that would be the end of him. His answer took me by surprise, and I've remembered it all these years. He told me that he wasn't worried about death, because it would just return him to the state in which he existed before he was born: that is, a state of complete nothingness. Well, if you really think about nirvana—or *moksha*, as the Hindus call it—it also returns us to a time when we had no self."

"That sounds like bliss to me," said Elaine.

"I understand fully what you're saying, Elaine, and there have been many times in my life when I would have jumped at that kind of bliss. At Houston Christian University, I teach classes on Romantic poetry. Romantic poets such as Samuel Taylor Coleridge, Lord Byron, Percy Bysshe Shelley, and John Keats often yearned for a cessation of thought, for an end to the over-self-consciousness that tormented them so. But I would suggest that we are not at our best when we yearn for the annihilation of our selfhood. We were created for more than that. I believe that when we are most worthy of ourselves and of our God-given humanity, we yearn for wholeness and integrity, the perfecting of our sinful selves."

"There is something in what you say, but why can't Buddha lead us to that wholeness as well as Christ?"

"Because only Christ rose bodily from the dead. Only Christ possesses within himself the eternal, uncreated life that we need if we are to defeat Satan, sin, and death. The eightfold noble path of Buddha is a noble one indeed, and I've been impressed, Elaine, by your discipline and the calmness of your spirit. But the teachings of sages and holy men can only take us so far. Remember what I said before dinner. There have been many great guides and prophets who have taught us a good and noble way to live our lives, but only Jesus claimed to be himself the Way (Jn 14:6)."

"Does that mean the East is wrong and the West is right?"

"Definitely not. A long line of holy men and prophets from West and East alike have taught reincarnation, the one soul, and the extinction, or at least controlling, of desire. And many who have followed them, both in the East and the West, have lived better lives and found peace and equanimity. The question is not whether the East or the West succeeded better in achieving that peace: Both have done so in their own way.

"No, there is only one question that really matters: Who was Jesus? Jesus, who lived his life in the middle lands between the East and the West, claimed to be more than a prophet or holy man: to have life in himself and to be able to share that life with others. Now, Elaine, if it could be proven that Christ did not rise from the dead, then I think the way of Buddhism is the best way of dealing with the universe in which we find ourselves. But if Jesus did rise from the dead—and I hope I have presented some good reasons to believe that he did—then everything changes."

"Are you saying if Jesus did not rise from the dead, you would be a Buddhist?"

"Well, yes and no. Were I a man of the East, I would be a Buddhist. However, since I am a man of the West, I would be a Stoic. Both systems of thought and of life are strikingly similar. They would present, I believe, the best religious and philosophical option if Jesus were simply one more prophet teaching a better way of living.

"Let's face it, folks, if Jesus wasn't who he claimed to be, if he was only a prophet who did and taught good things rather than the Son of God who died and rose again, then God has never *really* spoken—at least not in the way we so desperately need him to. Yes, he gave us his law and prophets to guide us, but if he doesn't love us enough to come to us, then we are finally alone in this world. And if we are alone, then we had best suck it up and live the disciplined, desire-avoiding life of the Buddhist or the Stoic."

"Louis," said Ali, "I like what you're saying, but I don't see how it relates to heaven and Jesus being the only way to get there."

"Too often we ask questions like that in the abstract. When we do, it makes Christianity sound like an elitist religion that thinks it is all right and every other religion is all wrong. But we can't even ask the question until we can determine, as we have been trying to do, what it means to go to heaven and what it means to be saved. Ali, would you mind if I bring up Spinoza again?"

"Absolutely not! The more Spinoza, the better!"

"There is a part of Spinoza I know you like, though you might be surprised to find that I like it too. Spinoza criticizes Jews and Christians who love and serve God only so they can win his favor and secure their place in heaven."

"Spinoza is right, but how can you agree with him?"

"Because the type of people Spinoza criticizes imagine, falsely, that getting into heaven is like getting an A in class rather than an F."

"Isn't it?"

"No, going to heaven is not like passing a class or winning the lottery or having all your theories proved right. Going to heaven means being with God for all eternity. Someone who was mercenary, who thought he could trick God into letting him into heaven, would not want to be in heaven—for being in heaven means being in perpetual communion with God and worshiping him forever.

"Christ is the only way to heaven, for being in heaven *means* being with Christ. To enter heaven is to enter into eternal life, but that life resides only in Christ, the one who is himself the way, the truth, and the life (Jn 14:6). If Christ really is the life, then to be outside him must necessarily be death."

"So you *are* saying that Christians are right and everyone else is wrong?"

"No, I'm saying that Christ is who he claimed to be."

"But you *do* believe that only Christians are going to heaven."

"I believe that to be in heaven means to be with Christ, and therefore a person can't go to heaven unless he is in Christ."

"I think you're being evasive."

"Perhaps I am, Ali, but I am trying to avoid falling into the trap of an agnostic friend of mine who also wrestled with Christianity's claim to be the only way."

"What trap is that?"

"Well, I spoke with my friend for thirty minutes, during which time he gave me all his reasons for hating the God revealed in the Bible. After he was done, he then added with a burst of indignation: 'And another thing I don't like about Christianity is that it teaches that non-Christians are going to hell!'"

"Where is the trap in that?"

"Without realizing it, my friend had contradicted himself. In his anger against Christians who say that non-Christians are going to hell, he forgot that being in heaven means spending eternity with the very God he had already told me he hated. That is why we can't speak of going to heaven in abstract terms. When we do that, we fall back into the false analogy that heaven means graduating and hell means failing."

"I still don't see what's wrong with that analogy."

"The problem with it is that it suggests there is only one college when there are in fact two: a college of heaven and a college of hell. Those who attend the former want to spend all eternity with the God who revealed himself most fully in Christ; those who attend the latter want to spend eternity with themselves, whether that means clinging to their sins or to their own sense of self-righteousness."

"Are you saying that people choose to go to hell?"

"Yes, in the end, it is we who make that choice."

"But how is that possible? Why would anyone choose hell?"

"Because we all want to be in control, to call the shots. That is just as true, if not more true, of religious people. Jesus himself says that there will be many in the last days who will boast that they prophesied and did miracles and cast out demons in his name, but Christ will say to them: 'I never knew you; depart from me, you workers of lawlessness' (Mt 7:23). Jesus speaks here of people who profess to be Christians, to be followers of Christ, but who have not surrendered their lives to him."

"Did Jesus really say that?"

"He did. In fact, that warning appears at the very end of his Sermon on the Mount. Well, almost the end. After Jesus issues that sober warning, he concludes his longest recorded sermon by saying that those who listen and heed his words are like people who build their home on the rock, while those who do not heed are like those who build on sand. When the rains fall and the floods rise, those founded on the rock will survive, while those on the sand will be washed away (Mt 7:24-27)."

"I seem to remember hearing a priest say once that Jesus did not come to bring peace but a sword."

"Yes, Jesus did say that (Mt 10:34), not because he was a warmonger but because his word is like a double-edged sword that cuts both ways (Heb 4:12). One cannot be neutral about Christ. Oh, we can be nominal Christians, taking some parts and leaving out others; but about Christ himself, we must either fall at his feet and worship him or hold him forever at arm's length. We don't do him any favors by praising his preaching and his meekness while ignoring the claims he made about himself.

"If Jesus is truly the Son of God who died for our sins and rose again, then he *must* be the only way. If he is not, if there are other ways to God, then that means God sent his Son into the world to die a painful and humiliating death to give us another option. It is not the Christian church that is the one way to God. The church is human and fallible and has often done terrible things. Still, God has entrusted the church, imperfect as it is, with the good news about Jesus. It is the doorway to salvation because it is the doorway to the one who is the Way."

"But what about Islam? Are you saying that Muslims are going to hell?"

"Reza," I said slowly, after shooting a quick prayer to God to guide my tongue as I took up so delicate a matter, "I am glad you did not ask this question at the beginning of our Thanksgiving dinner. I am glad we have already broken bread together and spoken with each other so honestly and sincerely and compassionately. I would like to continue now in that same tone of honesty, sincerity, and compassion."

"Please do," said Reza. "I would like to hear what is on your heart."

"Reza, let me begin by saying how much respect I have for the Muslim people as a whole. In the midst of a society that has lost its moral center and that has ceased to hold up the family as the bedrock of civilization, the majority of Muslims have continued to uphold the sacred relationship between husband and wife and parents and children and to live their lives in keeping with a fixed code of morality."

"Thank you for saying that. Many in the West today want to judge all Muslims by the evil acts of a handful of fanatics and terrorists."

"They are wrong to do so, Reza. They are also wrong when they say the Qur'an speaks only of violence and conquest. In fact, modern Christians who want to focus only on God's forgiveness and ignore his holiness would do well to read the Qur'an, for it holds God's wrath and mercy in a proper and healthy balance. The Qur'an reminds its readers again and again of the coming day of judgment and of the need for repentance. Like the law of Moses, it upholds justice and charity to the orphan and the widow and displays common sense in dealing with legal matters and covenants. It also, contrary to popular opinion, treats women with respect and gentleness. Most importantly of all, it calls on its readers to forsake all idols and to show gratitude to God."

"I'm so glad that you have seen those things in the Qur'an. And yet you seem to believe that there is something missing in Islam that is unique to Christianity."

"I do, Reza. The Qur'an speaks often and beautifully about the mercy of God, but never once does it say he is a God of love."

"But aren't love and mercy the same thing?"

"They are related, but they are not the same. Mercy allows us to forgive, but it is only by means of love that we can truly move out of ourselves toward another person. The God of the Qur'an is a distant God; we can serve and obey him, but we cannot know him intimately. Allah promises his followers a place in paradise, but he does not promise that he will be with them in paradise. Heaven in the Qur'an is a final reward, but it offers no union between God and man. There is nothing in the Qur'an like the great marriage of Christ and the church that the Bible promises, for Allah is utterly unknowable. He is, if I may express it that way, a lonely, isolated God."

"But isn't the Christian God also lonely and isolated?"

"No, he is not, for the God revealed in the Bible has always existed as the Trinity. Even before he created the universe, there was love within the Godhead, for the Father loves the Son eternally, and the Son loves the Father eternally. And that love is so rich and real and tangible that it is itself a person: the Holy Spirit. That's the beautiful way that C. S. Lewis, following in the footsteps of Saint Augustine, describes it in a book he wrote called *Mere Christianity*: the same book where he says that Jesus was either a liar, a lunatic, or the Lord."

"But the Qur'an denies the Trinity?"

"It does, Reza, but I believe that the reason Muhammad rejected the central Christian teaching of the Trinity is that he did not understand it."

"On what do you base that rather strong claim?"

"Stacey, can you please bring me my copy of—"

"Way ahead of you, Dad," she said as she handed me my copy of the Qur'an.

"Once again, Stacey, I'm forced to admit that you are a most excellent daughter!"

"We aims to please!"

"Reza," I said, flipping to sura 5, "I would like to read to you a passage from the Qur'an that is too often overlooked: 'When God says, "Jesus, son of Mary, did you say to people, 'Take me and my mother as two gods alongside God'?" he will say, "May you be exalted! I would never say what I had no right to say—if I had said any such thing You would have known it: You know all that is within me, though I do not know what is within You, You alone have full knowledge of things unseen—I told them only what You commanded me to: 'Worship God, my Lord and your Lord'"' (5:116-17)."

"Why do you highlight that passage?"

"Because in it, Muhammad clearly rejects the notion that Jesus and Mary are equally God alongside Allah. But the only reason he would go out of his way to reject it is if he thought there were people teaching that Allah, Jesus, and Mary were all equal gods. But the only people who would make such a claim would be the Christians. Of course, this is not what Christianity means when it speaks of the Trinity, but it seems clear to me that Muhammad thought it was. Now, if that *is* what Christians meant by the Trinity, then Muhammad would have been correct to reject that idea, but that is not what they meant. The Trinity is not God, Mary, and Jesus but God the Father, Jesus the Son, and the Holy Spirit."

"But why is it so important to believe that Jesus is the Son of God? Isn't it enough to believe he was a great prophet?"

"It's not enough, Reza. At the core of the Qur'an is the belief that God sent a prophet to all the various nations. For Muslims, Muhammad is the unique prophet sent to the Arabs. I have no problem with that basic concept, for it does seem that all nations have been blessed with at least one prophet or holy man who taught them the law and encouraged them to follow it. But if that is the case, and Jesus is only a prophet, then we don't really need him. The problem with man is not that we don't know the law; the problem is that we don't follow it. If we are to be saved from our sins, we need more than a prophet; we need God himself to come to earth and repair the brokenness."

"These are strong things you are saying. It is hard for a Muslim to imagine God being three and yet also one; even more, it is hard to imagine God dying."

"Reza, I believe you are a Shia rather than a Sunni Muslim. Is that correct?"

"It is. Why do you ask?"

"Because my study of Islam has led me to believe that a Shia can understand Christianity better than a Sunni."

"Why do you say that?"

"Let me try to explain it step by step. One thing I found a bit disturbing when I read the Qur'an was the way Muhammad made slight changes to Bible stories so as to prevent the prophets of God from suffering or being falsely accused. For example, in the Bible, Joseph is falsely accused by Potiphar's wife and thrown in jail (Gen 39), but in sura 12, Muhammad has Potiphar show up and declare Joseph innocent. After that, Joseph is put in prison, but only to protect him, not to punish him. The same holds for Moses and other prophets. In fact, much to my surprise, Abel never appears on the various lists of prophets scattered throughout the Qur'an (4:163, for example). I can only theorize Abel is not on any of the lists because he was killed by his brother Cain."

"I never thought about it that way, but you are correct."

"Reza, these changes are only minor ones, but, when it gets to Jesus, the Qur'an says that Jesus never actually died on the cross (4:156-60). Because Jesus is a prophet, the Qur'an will not let him suffer and die for our sins. But that is problematic. In the Qur'an, two things are made clear: first, that Jesus was a prophet; second, as we discussed earlier, that the Torah and the Gospels are revelation from God (3:2-4)."

"Why is that a problem?"

"In the Gospels, Jesus prophesies three times that he will go to Jerusalem, where he will suffer, be mocked, rejected, beaten, and killed—but then rise again on the third day (Lk 9:22, 44; 18:31-32). If he was not actually killed in Jerusalem, then that means he prophesied falsely about himself, but if he is a true prophet, as the Qur'an says, then all his prophecies must come true—for a prophet who makes a prophecy that does not come true must, by definition, be a false prophet."

"That is a powerful argument that I need to think about some more. But what does that have to do with my being a Shia?"

"Reza, I believe the Shia have a fuller appreciation for suffering than the Sunni because they hold in high honor the assassination of Ali, an evil act that was perpetrated against a righteous man of God and the true successor of Muhammad. Because of their understanding of the way Ali was rejected, slandered, and killed, I believe the Shia are better able to understand how it is that God would allow Jesus to be rejected, slandered, and killed as a means of cleansing us from our sin and opening the gates of heaven."

"Lou, I think my mind is about to explode with all these new ideas. I'll have to mull these things over for a few weeks and then get back to you."

"Please take your time!"

"But I did have one other question? Why is it that—"

Reza never finished asking his question, for, before he could speak another word, all the lights in the house went out, and the dining room was plunged into darkness.

9

WHAT ABOUT THE PEOPLE WHO LIVED BEFORE CHRIST?

"ELAINE," I SAID, removing the pack of matches that I had put in the breast pocket of my shirt, "do you still have that candle?"

"Yes," she said.

"Wonderful," I replied as I struck the match, stretched my arm over toward Elaine, and touched the flame to the wick. Immediately the candle spluttered into life.

"Alex," I said, as my eyes slowly adjusted to the light, "please get the rest of the candles from the drawer in the hutch."

As he did that, I handed the pack of matches to Stacey.

"Now, children," I said, when everything was in place, "let there be light."

One by one, Alex and Stacey lit the candles until the dining room was bathed in a warm golden glow. In keeping with my Greek heritage, I had set up several icons on the hutch. As I stared at the icons through the candlelight, I was reminded that icons are best seen through a gently flickering flame. Seen in that light and from that perspective, the icon better serves its purpose of flattening out time and space so as to give the viewer a glimpse of eternity.

In many ways, I had already caught such a glimpse in the conversations of the last several hours. *Heaven*, I thought to myself, *will be much like this blessed Thanksgiving dinner*—a feast of fellowship with people from every tribe and nation and tongue.

"My friends," I said, "the world lost something beautiful and fragile when electric lights were invented. I'd forgotten how magical candlelight can be. Alex and Stacey, can you share with our guests what I taught you about magic when you were little?"

"The world is full of magic," said Alex with a smile.

"We just have to have eyes to see it," added Stacey, "and ears to hear it."

"You two bring joy to your father's heart! The world is indeed full of magic, but in all the hustle and bustle, we miss it. We grow blind and deaf without even knowing it. But light a candle in a dark room and watch as the golden flame draws out from every human face its worries and its hopes, its cares and its dreams. Watch the flickering play of light and shadow, and see in it the story of our lives and of the lives of the whole human race. So much promise allied with so much folly, such brief and poignant joy, such sad misfortune and grievous loss."

"Louis," said Ali, "if we were in Germany, I would say you were suffering from *Sehnsucht*."

"It's funny you should say that, Ali. C. S. Lewis used that very German word to describe the feelings of longing and yearning he felt when he was a boy: yearnings for something beyond the world, for something nature could not supply. It was those desires, in great part, that led him to Jesus."

"You speak of desire," said Ali, "but what good is desire if you can't find an object for that desire? When you said earlier that Christ was the only way to God, you forgot to take into account the millions of people who lived on the earth before Jesus was born. Must they all go to hell because they were born at the wrong time?"

"Ali, before we face that question head-on, I want to share something I have struggled with for much of my life. In the same way you have struggled with Jewish claims to chosenness, I have struggled with a related issue surrounding those claims. Could it really be that before the birth of Christ, God ignored 99 percent of the world and cared only for the Jews? Did God really leave everyone but the children of Israel in the dark? That doesn't seem consistent with God's character."

"Exactly! Now you are talking sense!"

"I'm glad you approve! But, after spending many years studying the Bible and Christian theology, I realized that God was not silent all those years. He did speak to the Gentile nations but in a different way."

"Different in what way?"

"Theologians make a vital distinction between general revelation and special revelation. General revelation refers to the way God speaks to all people through nature and through their conscience. Special revelation refers to those times when God speaks directly through his prophets, through the law he gave to Moses, through the inspired writers of the Bible, and, supremely, through his Son."

"Wait a minute," said Bill, "are those just ideas thought up by theologians, or is that distinction in the Bible?"

"It is in the Bible, Bill, most clearly in Paul's letter to the church at Rome. In the first chapter of Romans, Paul says that the Gentiles who live lives of sin are without excuse for God's glory and power are clearly seen in creation (Rom 1:18-23). That is to say, though they lack special revelation, they can perceive and know God's majesty by studying the universe and the natural world.

"Then, in the second chapter, he says clearly that the Gentiles who do not know the law of Moses are a law unto themselves, for God's standards are written in their heart—that is to say, their conscience (Rom 2:12-16). Now, nature and conscience cannot, in and of themselves, teach a person about the Trinity or that Jesus is the Son of God. But general revelation does point to a God outside the physical, material realm who can be known and who expects us to live by certain standards."

"You're quoting from the New Testament," said Bill, "but what about the Old Testament? Is the same distinction made there as well?"

"It is made most clearly in Psalm 19, which begins with the wonderful verse: 'The heavens declare the glory of God.' The first half of the psalm (Ps 19:1-6) extols God's glory as it is displayed for all to see in the heavens. But then, starting at Psalm 19:7, it moves away from nature and celebrates God's law. Now, in the first half of the psalm, when the focus is on general revelation as seen in nature, the psalmist uses a generic name for 'God,' similar to the English word *God*, which is used by people from all different religions. However, when he switches to celebrate the special revelation that only comes to us though God's revealed law, he uses God's personal, covenant name, the one he revealed to Moses at the burning bush: I am that I am, or *Yahweh*, which English Bibles translate as Lord written in small caps."

"I still don't see," said Ali, "how these Bible passages address the question of why God spoke to the Jews and ignored everyone else."

"What they are saying, Ali, is that God did not ignore the Gentiles; he just spoke to them in a more generic way. Remember what we discussed between dinner and dessert: that God decided to focus on the Jews as a way of keeping his law pure and protecting the bloodline of the promised Messiah. So, yes, God spoke directly only to the Jews."

"Wait a minute, Dr. Markos," said David, "some of the prophets, like Jonah, did speak the word of God directly to some of the Gentiles."

"Good point, David! It is true that the Jewish prophets were often sent by God to warn the Gentile nations. I suppose it would be more accurate to say that God spoke only to the Jews directly as part of a special covenant relationship."

"Ah," said Ali, "there is that chosenness again!"

"Yes," I admitted, "it is unescapable. Still, although God's covenant relationship was unique, he did not hide himself from all the other nations. He poured out knowledge about himself in a more indirect way through the general revelation of nature and conscience. And, I would add, one other way as well."

"What other way is that?"

"Through their stories and myths, their magical rites and sacred rituals. True, many of those myths and rituals were bloody and savage, but they all speak in unison of our human need for forgiveness and expiation of sin."

"Did the pagan nations really have a notion of sin?"

"Good point, Ali! It is true that they didn't have a clear understanding of sin in the way that Jews, Christians, and Muslims do, because they lacked an all-holy God against whom to measure it. And yet, they all understood that there are taboo crimes that render us, as individuals and as communities, unclean and in need of some kind of sacrifice to bring us back into a right relationship with the spiritual realm."

"Like in Greek tragedy? It was through a Greek tragedy that you adapted into English that we first met."

"It was, Ali, and we've been discussing the big questions of life ever since! Most of the heroes in the plays of Aeschylus, Sophocles, and Euripides are scapegoats who must suffer to restore balance and health to their kingdoms. In this great task, the gods could offer little help, for the gods of Greek mythology were anything but holy. Still, the tragedies cry out for gods who will bridge the gap, who will combine love and compassion with wrath and judgment. The pagans did not know such a God, but they yearned for him."

"What about the philosophers?"

"I'm glad you asked that. To really see how God spoke, dimly and indistinctly, to the ancient pagans of Greece and Rome, we must combine the witness of the myth makers and the philosophers. While the common people gravitated toward rituals through which to appease the gods, the philosophers sought after a higher, more removed God who did not change or display human emotions. They did not think to combine this dual witness of heart and head, imagination and reason, intuition and logic."

"Dad," said Alex, "tell Ali about what Chesterton says about the shepherds and the wise men in the nativity story."

"Excellent suggestion, Alex. I'm so glad you have continued your reading of *The Everlasting Man*. In that wonderful book, which demands at least two or three readings, G. K. Chesterton makes an argument I have never forgotten. He reminds his readers that in the ancient world, religion and philosophy were very much separate pursuits. Those who joined mystery cults and shivered in numinous awe before the tales of Zeus and Athena and Apollo tended to be from the countryside and from the lower echelons of society. Those who joined the Stoics or Epicureans or Neoplatonists and thought the pursuit of ethics more important than miraculous stories about gods and goddesses tended to be rich, urban, and highly educated."

"I like the second group more than the first."

"I myself gravitate that way as well, Ali, until something happens that I cannot explain with logic and reason, and then the old pagan inside awakens and begins his search for that wonder and magic that lightens up this cold, weary world with life and meaning."

"Louis, are you a professor or a poet, a philosopher or a pagan?"

"A little bit of both, I suppose. Either side alone is insufficient. The head needs the heart as much as the heart needs the head. For Chesterton, heart and head finally came together at the foot of the manger, when rude, primitive shepherds knelt down beside the urbane, sophisticated wise men. Both were drawn to the most wonderful, most audacious miracle in the history of the world, the one that defied all human logic and surpassed the wildest dreams of the pagans. Here, in a feeding trough, the omnipotent, omniscient, omnipresent God of the philosophers becomes one with the poorest of the poor. Here, if we will only have eyes to see and ears to hear, lies the greatest magic of all."

"You *are* a poet, my friend, a poet and a dreamer."

"Perhaps, Ali, though I think the candlelight is partly to blame. Seen through the dance of that candle's golden flame, my icon of the resurrection appears to hover between the fairy world of myth and the factual world of history. You see, when my kids were young, I always told them stories before putting them to sleep. Sometimes the stories came from Greek mythology; other times they came from the Bible. One evening, the kids asked me what the relationship was between the myths and the Bible. Alex, do you remember my answer?"

"Of course I do," said Alex. "You said Greek mythology was like a candle, and the Bible was like the sun. I wrote a paper about that very subject in college. In it, I quoted Clement of Alexandria's *Exhortation to the Heathen*. Clement echoes Paul's speech at the Areopagus (Acts 17), where he tells his Athenian audience that he will reveal to them the true identity of the unknown God they have worshiped. Clement explains to his own pagan audience that if they had read their own myths closely enough, they would have seen in them intimations of the truth to come. I remember that he *does* mock those stories a bit roughly, but he nevertheless shows how they point to Christ."

"Well said, Alex! And do you remember what you learned about yourself by writing that essay?"

"Yes! I realized that I had believed in Jesus as a myth long before I believed in him as a fact."

"Thanks for sharing that, Alex! The sun's power to illuminate far exceeds that of a lowly candle, but what a blessing a candle is in a darkened room. For thousands of years, those who had no access to God's special revelation were guided by the candles of their myths and epics and tragedies. But a time came when they were invited to exchange their candles for the full revelation of the sun."

"Are you saying that Jesus Christ is Santa Claus for adults?"

"I must say, Ali, that you do a wonderful job of keeping me on my toes. I guess what my son and I just said about myth and fact, candle and sun, might suggest that Christianity is nothing more than a sophisticated myth. But that is because there is some real truth in that statement."

"Are you agreeing that Jesus is Santa for adults?"

"No, not in the literal sense, but I am agreeing that Jesus appeals as much to our need for myth as to our need for fact."

"What's the difference?"

I paused for a moment to collect my thoughts and then asked everyone at the table a question that took them by surprise.

"Did any of you notice a common theme in the den?"

After a few moments of silence, Anthony laughed and spoke: "How could we miss it? You have a movie poster from *The Lion, the Witch and the Wardrobe* and several large maps from *The Lord of the Rings*."

"I hope you didn't miss the rug with the map of Middle-earth on it?" Alex added.

"How could I?" said Anthony. "My feet were resting in Mordor for ten minutes!"

"I'm so glad you all noticed," I said with pride. "The posters and maps pay homage to my love for C. S. Lewis and J. R. R. Tolkien as well as to the friendship they shared. In fact, Lewis might never have become a Christian were it not for Tolkien."

"How so?" asked Ali.

"Although Lewis became the greatest Christian apologist of the twentieth century, he spent the first half of his life as an atheist. After a long search and the intervention of some Christian friends and colleagues, Lewis accepted that God existed, but he still found himself unable to believe that Jesus was the Son of God."

"I'd be interested to know what was stopping him."

"As it turns out, Ali, the stumbling block for Lewis was the very issue of myth we have been discussing. Like me, Lewis was an English professor who loved myth and who eagerly sought connections between the stories and rituals of various primitive religions. With the help of *The Golden Bough* of Sir James Frazer, he came to identify an archetype known as the Corn King that appears in various guises in the myths of such diverse people groups as the Greeks, the Romans, the Norsemen, the Egyptians, the Babylonians, and the Persians."

"I'm not familiar with the Corn King myth. Can you describe it?"

"Well, as we discussed earlier, almost all pagan nations share a sense of taboo guilt that must be expiated. The Corn King is a semidivine figure who enters our world as a kind of bridge between heaven and earth. Despite his powers, he is inevitably killed, often by treachery; but his death does not mark an end to his story. In some way or other, he rises again, bringing hope and promise to his followers. He is called the Corn King because his dying and rising ends up being linked to the seasonal cycle of life, death, and rebirth, of sowing and reaping, of autumn and spring. He goes by such names as Osiris, Adonis, Tammuz, Mithras, and Balder."

"But that sounds just like the myth of Jesus."

"That's exactly what Lewis thought. He took for granted that the gospel of Jesus' birth, death, and resurrection was nothing more than the Hebrew version of the same ancient Corn King myth. He simply couldn't see what the death of an obscure Jewish rabbi could mean to somebody living in the modern world."

"That sounds logical to me. What changed his mind?"

"None other than the author of *The Lord of the Rings*. Tolkien, a strong Catholic, had been friends and colleagues with Lewis for five years but had proven unable to break through Lewis's thick atheist shell. One night, as they strolled along the grounds of Magdalen College, Oxford, they discussed the similarities between the Corn King myth and the Christian gospel. Up until that point, Lewis had convinced himself that Jesus was merely one of many cultural incarnations of the age-old Corn King. On that special evening, Tolkien gently nudged Lewis to reinterpret his reading of Jesus and the Corn King."

"What other reading could there be?"

"That the reason Jesus sounds so much like a myth is that he was the myth that came true."

"It sounds to me like we're back to Santa Claus."

"Santa Claus is a legendary reworking of a real, historical man named Saint Nicholas. Jesus is quite the opposite. He is the real, historical Son of God through whom God satisfied the primal needs for which the mythic stories of Osiris and Adonis, Mithras and Balder were but a shadowy expression. Christians have always recognized Jesus as the fulfillment of the Old Testament Law and Prophets. What Tolkien helped Lewis to see is that Jesus also fulfilled the deepest yearnings of the pagan peoples.

"Think about it. If the gospel story were totally foreign to the myths and rituals of 99 percent of the human population, then it would seem as if a foreign god had invaded our earth. But that is not what happened. Just as the Jewish converts to Christianity discerned in Jesus their long-awaited Messiah, so the Gentile converts discerned in him the Corn King come to life."

"Are you sure the Bible says any of this?" asked Bill.

"I believe it does, Bill. In fact, I think there is a passage in the Gospel of John where Jesus himself makes the connection."

"Where's that?"

"In John 12, some Greeks who are in Jerusalem to celebrate the Passover approach Philip, a Jewish disciple of Jesus who bears a Greek name, and ask whether they can have a meeting with Jesus. Philip carries the message to Jesus, who replies with these words: 'The hour has come for the Son of Man to be glorified. Truly, truly, I say to you, unless a grain of wheat falls into the earth and dies, it remains alone; but if it dies, it bears much fruit' (Jn 12:23-24)."

"I've heard that verse before, but what does it have to do with Jesus building a bridge between himself and the myths of the Greeks?"

"To answer that question, Bill, I need to argue for something that is admittedly speculative. Although the Bible passage does not tell us anything more about the Greeks, it is clear they are interested in the Jewish ritual of the Passover. I would theorize that the Greeks were members of the most ancient and honored cult in the Greek world, one that Caesar Augustus himself respected. That cult was known as the Eleusinian mysteries, for it met near Athens in the town of Eleusis.

"Though we don't know as much as we would like to know about this secret cult, we do know that they worshiped the goddess Persephone and the god Bacchus, both of whose worship was linked to the seasonal cycle of the wheat—or corn, to use the British word for "wheat"—and of the grape. We also know that they had an altar on which they would put a ripe ear of wheat."

"That sounds like the Corn King myth we have been discussing," said Ali.

"Exactly. The Eleusinians clearly found hope for salvation in the pattern of life, death, and resurrection from which they secured their bread and their wine."

"But what makes you believe the Greeks in the story were from Eleusis?" asked Bill, who was a bit suspicious about my reading of the passage.

"Because the image or metaphor that Jesus uses about the grain of wheat that is buried and dies but that bears much fruit is *not* a Jewish one. The image does not appear in the Old Testament, and it is never used by Jesus in any of his parables. The image, however, is one that Greeks from Eleusis would immediately recognize. It is as if Jesus is saying to them: 'For generations, you have been worshiping the seed that dies and is reborn; I *am* that seed, and through my death, I will bring new life into the world.'

"Do you see the implication here? Jesus is the Corn King come true: not some myth taking place nobody knows when but a real, historical man who died and rose again in the city of Jerusalem while Tiberius was emperor, Pontius Pilate was the Roman governor, and Herod Antipas was the Jewish king."

"That is a beautiful story," said Ali, "but is it true, or just your own idea?"

"Ali, I must admit that I've not encountered any other theologian who makes this exact connection. I do think my argument makes sense and fits well with the facts that we have, but, again, it is not the common reading of the story. Still, there is another passage in the Bible that makes a similar connection that is widely recognized and accepted by theologians and Bible scholars. In fact, Alex has already alluded to it!"

"Let's hear it!" said Ali and Bill at once.

"During his second missionary journey, Paul, God's self-appointed missionary to the Gentiles, finds himself in the agora, the ancient marketplace of Athens. At first, he is troubled by the scores of idols that greet him. But then his eye falls on one particular temple that bears the inscription 'To an Unknown God.' When he sees that, he requests an audience with the Areopagus, a group that used to make political laws but, by the first century AD, had become more of a cultural board for the purpose of censoring or allowing in new religious ideas.

"Rather than stand before the Areopagus and criticize them for their idolatry, Paul calls them a religious people and then highlights the temple he saw to the unknown God. It is then that Paul speaks the words that I believe the entire Greco-Roman world was waiting to hear:

> What therefore you worship as unknown, this I proclaim to you. The God who made the world and everything in it, being Lord of heaven and earth, does not live in temples made by man, nor is he served by human hands, as though he needed anything, since he himself gives to all mankind life and breath and everything. And he made from one man every nation of mankind to live on all the face of the earth, having determined allotted periods and the boundaries of their dwelling place, that they should seek God, and perhaps feel their way toward him and find him. Yet he is actually not far from each one of us, for
>
> "In him we live and move and have our being,"
>
> as even some of your own poets have said,
>
> "For we are indeed his offspring." (Acts 17:23-28)

"When Paul says, 'your own poets,' he means pagan Greek poets who lived centuries before Jesus. One poet, named Epimenides, wrote, 'In him we live and move and have our being'; another, named Aratus, wrote, 'For we are indeed his offspring.' Although, in both lines of poetry, the 'him'/'his' refers to Zeus, Paul treats the poems as if they were inspired by the God of the Bible. Or, to put it another way, Paul interprets them as examples of general revelation that point the way to the special revelation of Christ and the New Testament."

"Louis," said Ali after reflecting for a moment, "I see now the point you are trying to make. But that point does not answer my initial question: What about the millions of people who died before Christ was born? None of them had the chance to hear Jesus speak of the seed that must die, or Paul speak of the unknown God. Must they therefore go to hell because they were born too early?"

"Ali, let me begin by admitting that no one can answer your question with 100 percent certainty. The Bible makes it clear that salvation is only through and in Christ, but it does not explain clearly how God deals with those Gentiles who lived before Jesus. There is, however, an intriguing verse in 1 Peter that offers a possible answer:

> For Christ also suffered once for sins, the righteous for the unrighteous, that he might bring us to God, being put to death in the flesh but made alive in the spirit, in which he went and proclaimed to the spirits in prison, because they formerly did not obey, when God's patience waited in the days of Noah, while the ark was being prepared, in which a few, that is, eight persons, were brought safely through water. (1 Pet 3:18-20)

"Now this is not an easy passage to interpret, but it seems to suggest that between his death and resurrection, Jesus descended into hell and preached to those who were killed in Noah's flood. If Jesus did that, perhaps he preached to all those who died before his coming. Remember that the final judgment does not happen until the end of the world, when Christ returns. Remember also that once Jesus died, he stepped out of time into eternity. Perhaps in that eternal moment when he preached to the prisoners, all souls—past, present, and future—who died without having the chance to know Christ were given the opportunity to hear the good news."

"I do recall reciting the Apostles' Creed when I was a boy; it said that Christ descended into hell before he rose on the third day and ascended into heaven."

"Yes, that phrase, 'he descended into hell,' does appear in the Apostles' Creed. The event it points to is known as the harrowing of hell, for in his descent Christ broke down the gates of hell and rescued the righteous people of the Old Testament. Could it not be the case that when Jesus rescued Adam and Eve, Abraham and Sarah, Moses and Elijah, David and Daniel, he also held out his hands to Gentiles who had no access to the special revelation of the Jewish Law and Prophets?"

"That sounds a bit speculative, doesn't it?" said Bill.

"Yes, Bill, it is speculative, but I think it fits with the character of God and with the whole sacred narrative of the Bible. But there is another version of this speculative argument that I believe answers even more questions. You probably won't be surprised to find that I learned it from my mentor, C. S. Lewis!"

"No surprise there! But tell us what Lewis says."

"Perhaps those who never had the chance in life to hear the good news about Jesus' crucifixion and resurrection are given that chance at the moment of their death. That is to say, when they die, Christ appears to them and offers them salvation."

"But I thought Christianity teaches that once a person dies all bets are off, that if you die an unbeliever, you go to hell."

"Yes, Bill, that's the teaching of the church, but, as Lewis reminds us, we forget that the moment of our death is an eternal moment. Once we die, we step out of time into eternity, into a dimension in which it is always now. In a way that we time-trapped creatures cannot fully understand, that eternal moment contains every moment—and every choice—of our life on the earth.

"Could it not be that Christ meets us in that eternal moment in such a way that, if all our actions and choices on earth were leading us in the direction of obedience, love, and adoration of the Creator, we will accept Christ as the proper end and fulfillment of all those actions and choices? Although, technically speaking, that sounds like postmortem salvation, it is really an acknowledgment that God made us for eternity and that when we step into eternity, all we were in time comes to a climax. Might God not meet us at that moment of climax, allowing us to either receive or reject his grace? True, the decision itself will take place after death, but it will be the fruit of a life lived in time."

"I must say I like this suggestion," said Ali.

"I do as well, not only because it helps answer your question about those who lived before Christ but because it also helps answer the related question: What happens to those who lived after Christ but never had a chance to hear the gospel?"

"Yes, I can see that."

"It also answers a second, related question that has troubled me in the past. I often worry about that proverbial man in the middle of Africa or Asia who dies without the opportunity to accept or reject the grace of Christ. But I worry as well about the many people in America who also lack that opportunity, not because they've never heard the gospel but because they have grown up in a home or a community in which every single association with Christianity has been hypocritical, manipulative, and abusive. I would argue that, for such a person, acceptance of Jesus might be psychologically impossible.

"But, if Christ does indeed appear to such people in the moment of their death, then maybe, just maybe, in that glorious moment of meeting, all the hypocrisy, manipulation, and abuse that has twisted them away from God will fall away like dross, leaving behind a golden glow of peace and clarity. Only then, when all the junk, all the baggage, has been washed away, will they be able to see and understand clearly what Christ's offer of grace means and thus be able to make a true and free decision."

"That's quite beautiful," said Sita, who had been listening intently to my dialogue with Ali and Bill.

"I really do believe it is, Sita, and though I can't prove it, I can at least offer an illustration from the Bible that parallels what I pray will happen to us all at the moment of our death. I speak of my favorite part of the Christmas story, the journey of the magi."

"I like that story as well," said Ali, "and it does seem an appropriate one since the people dining with us today come from all over the world."

"Amen to that, Ali! I think the magi would have felt quite welcome at our Thanksgiving dinner and that they would have heartily approved of your turkey!"

"Absolutely! They were men of fine and discerning taste!"

"We sometimes forget that the magi had no access to the Jewish Law or Prophets. In the absence of special revelation, they relied only on the general revelation they read in the heavens. They spent their lives studying the stars, and it was those stars that sent them on their long and probably dangerous journey. They did not know where the star would lead them, but lead them it did to the Christ child.

"Now, when the magi, exhausted from their journey, stood before the baby Jesus, they could have responded this way: 'You've got to be kidding! We came all this way for this, for a helpless baby born to poor parents. That's it? We're going home, and that's the last time we ever follow a stupid star.'"

"I could understand that reaction."

"So could I, Ali. It would have seemed a most appropriate response. But that is not what the magi said. What they said was this: 'Yes, this is what we have been searching for all our lives, though we never really knew it 'til now. We couldn't have guessed it, but now that we're here, we recognize that this is the one for whom we have waited and pined and yearned.' To borrow a line from my favorite Christmas carol, the hopes and fears of all the years were met that night in a stable in Bethlehem.

"I believe, or at least I hope, that all those who have never had a chance to know and to embrace the Christ child will find him at the end of their life's journey, in that magical moment-that-contains-all-other-moments that awaits us when we cross over from time into eternity. It will be then that all the magi of the world will have the chance to blow out their candles and look with wonder on the Risen Sun."

I would have said more, but before I could speak another word, the electricity came back on, and the dining room was flooded with light.

10

WHAT ABOUT NEW AGE SPIRITUALITY?

WHEN THE LIGHTS CAME BACK ON, I returned to my piano bench prepared to sing more hymns with the group, but my son, daughter, and the other college-age students insisted I play some Disney songs. Never one to turn down a chance to sing songs from those wonderful animated films that graced my childhood and that of my children, I opened up my Disney fake book and played our theme song: "A Whole New World."

I always chose randomly what song I would play next, but we invariably sung our way through "Can You Feel the Love Tonight," "Gaston," "Kiss the Girl," "I Won't Say I'm in Love," "Prince Ali," "Be Our Guest," "Part of Your World," "God Help the Outcast," "Once Upon a Dream," "Bella Notte," "The Bare Necessities," and "When You Wish upon a Star." My regulars not only knew all the words; they knew all the hand motions and ad-libs from the films as well.

As we paused to take a breath after singing fourteen songs back to back, Sita quietly asked whether we could sing "Colors of the Wind" from *Pocahontas*. I was happy to oblige, and the group sang the song with a mixture of gusto and reverential awe. We were all moved by the song's haunting call to "sing with all the voices of the mountains" and "paint with all the colors of the wind." For a moment, we all felt mystically "connected to each other, in a circle, in a hoop that never ends."

"I've always loved that song," said Sita in a hushed voice that was almost a whisper. "It makes me feel closer to nature and the spirit that runs through nature."

I was about to agree with her when Bill stood up and walked toward the piano. He had been dating a lovely Chinese woman who had been attracted to different aspects of Christianity, Hinduism, and Buddhism, and he had himself studied various forms of Eastern spirituality. "In all our discussions this evening about East and West," he said, "we have overlooked the possibility that the two can be combined."

"How do you mean?" I asked.

"Well," he said, "I'm thinking about all the beliefs and practices that Americans still group under the umbrella of New Age spirituality: crystals, automatic writing, astral projection, Wicca, séances, Ouija boards, transcendental meditation, astrology, and the occult. I admit that many of these have gotten commercialized and attract quacks and con artists, but many have their roots in respected and even scientific Eastern practices: acupuncture, chiropractic, herbal and holistic medicine, and martial arts. Most of these rely on a belief that patterns of energy known as chi run through our body."

"Bill," I replied, "you might be surprised to know that I agree with some of what you just said. Last year, our friend Ali convinced me to visit an acupuncturist whose needles not only helped relieve some of my stomach problems but cured Stewart's debilitating back problems. I believe that what the Chinese call chi (or qi) likely does exist, and, though I know many of my fellow Christians would disagree with me here, I do not think its existence is incompatible with the Bible."

"It's true," said Stewart, "it's true. All my Western doctors couldn't get me out of my wheelchair. Dr. Lee's magic needles got me walking again."

"Stewart and Louis," said Ali, "I'm glad you both took my advice."

"So am I!" I said. "Remember, Ali, when you got so filled up with qigong energy that you ran right into a tree?"

"How can I forget? It was like riding a horse!"

"In the Psalms, David says we are fearfully and wonderfully made (Ps 139:14), and I see no reason to doubt that God wove patterns of energy through our bodies and through the natural world. We must not forget that before Europe was secularized by the Enlightenment, Western medicine was also holistic. Instead of balancing chi, European doctors sought to balance the four humors, or liquids, that course their way through our circulatory and lymphatic system: blood, phlegm, bile, and black bile."

"That's true," said Anthony, who had read a bit about holistic medicine and was listening intently to our conversation. "Though medicine no longer speaks of the four humors, psychology still speaks of the four personality types that used to be linked to the humors: sanguine, phlegmatic, choleric, and melancholy."

"Exactly, Anthony!" I said with a look of professorial pride. "The four-humors theory of health gets a bad rap today because all people know about it is that doctors used to bleed people to restore the harmony of the humors—a process some historians argue hastened the death of George Washington!"

"That's unfortunate," said Anthony, "because the four humors, like chi, point to a vision of health that seems to have been lost in the West."

"What's that?" said Bill.

"That health consists in a proper balance of our physical and mental faculties."

"Well put, Anthony!" I exclaimed. "I could not have said it better myself. It gladdens my heart that young men with your wisdom are entering the medical field."

Anthony bowed his head slightly to conceal the blush that ran across his cheeks. He was a shy student and usually kept a low profile. His Egyptian background, like my own Greek background, had taught him that one should not dismiss traditional home remedies that rely on the healing powers of roots, herbs, and spices.

"It is only since the Enlightenment," I said, turning to face the group, "that the West chose to privilege analysis over synthesis, drugs and surgery over natural cures, compartmentalization over a holistic understanding of the human person. If you go to a Western doctor with back trouble, he will isolate your back from the rest of your body and perhaps perform surgery. If you go to a chiropractor, he will study your back in relation to the rest of your body and attempt to restore the lost balance that is causing the pain."

"Yes," said Anthony, "and if you asked each of the doctors what he thought about the other one, he would likely warn you not to listen to him!"

"Right again, Anthony! You see," I said, addressing everyone, "the difference here is not between West and East, or science and superstition, or Christianity and Buddhism. It is the difference between a modern and a traditional view of health and well-being. In the Middle Ages and the Renaissance, Christians believed that man represented in himself a microcosm of that greater macrocosm that is God's creation. There were connections and correspondences that ran between each part of our body and the body of the world."

"That sounds very Eastern," said Elaine, who appeared to be growing increasingly interested in our conversation.

"It does," I said. "Western Christians often forget that the relationship between Jesus and his disciples was less like that between a Western theology professor and his students and more like that between an Eastern martial arts sensei and his pupils."

"So," said Bill, with a touch of triumph in his voice, "you are saying that you think New Age spirituality is a good thing!"

Oh my, I thought to myself, *I walked right into that trap.*

After I had the chance to collect my thoughts and come up with a strategy for addressing Bill's question, I swung myself around to face the piano. Shooting up a silent prayer for divine assistance, I played a familiar melody with my right hand.

"Does anyone recognize that tune?"

"Of course," Alex said. "That's the Imperial March from *Star Wars*. It plays every time Darth Vader appears on the screen."

"Excellent, my son, I knew you wouldn't miss a John Williams motif. I'm sure most of you are familiar with the plot of *Star Wars* and of its central dogma that the Force, which binds all things in the universe, can be channeled for good or for evil."

Nearly everyone nodded in agreement, so I continued.

"On the one hand, George Lucas's treatment of the Force is incompatible with Christianity, for it suggests that God is an impersonal energy, like chi, that can be manipulated by human beings. And yet, on the other hand, it offers a warning that devotees of New Age spirituality would do well to heed."

"What's that?" asked Bill.

"That just because something is spiritual, it is not necessarily good. Stacey," I said, turning my head toward my daughter, "isn't there another line from *Fiddler on the Roof* that I remind you of now and then, a line from the song 'Matchmaker'?"

"I know what you mean, Dad," she sighed. "'Playing with matches a girl can get burned.'"

"Exactly! The one true God who created all things out of nothing made a host of spiritual beings we call angels. Although angels were created good, some of them fell and became what we call demons. Earlier this evening I critiqued two types of dualism: One posits an equally powerful good and evil god; the other treats the soul as all good and the body as all bad. But there is a third, lesser type of dualism that accurately defines the kind of world we live in: a world in which angelic and demonic forces war with each other. David, could you please read out loud for us Revelation 12:7-9?"

"Sure," he said and began to read the passage off his phone:

> Now war arose in heaven, Michael and his angels fighting against the dragon. And the dragon and his angels fought back, but he was defeated, and there was no longer any place for them in heaven. And the great dragon was thrown down, that ancient serpent, who is called the devil and Satan, the deceiver of the whole world—he was thrown down to the earth, and his angels were thrown down with him.

"Although John Milton's description of the rebellion of Satan in *Paradise Lost* plays fast and loose with the biblical texts, the Scriptures do make clear that angels and demons exist and that their struggles have repercussions on the earth and in our lives."

"Are you saying all New Age spirituality is demonic?"

"No, Bill, not all of it," I replied. "Some of it is based on Eastern understandings of health, medicine, and our relationship to the natural world that the West would do well to study. Much of it is pure charlatanism. But there are significant aspects of the New Age that I would not play around with."

"Like what, Lou?" asked Bill.

"I am a mature and sober-minded Christian, but I would never attend a séance or consult a medium or Ouija board lest I open myself up to unclean spirits. The Bible is clear that the devil prowls around like a roaring lion (1 Pet 5:8) and that we should not give him a foothold in our lives (Eph 4:27). When the devil appears, our job is to rebuke him in the name of Jesus and turn our attention back to God (Jas 4:7). When Jesus was tempted in the wilderness, he did not engage the devil in conversation but rebuked him using verses from Deuteronomy (Mt 4:1-11)."

"Are you then opposed to yoga and meditation?" asked Elaine.

"Elaine, great spiritual warriors of the Christian faith have practiced techniques of meditation for nearly two thousand years. Among the Greek Orthodox, the tradition in which I was raised, many priests, monks, and laymen practice the Jesus Prayer. As they breathe in through their nose and out through their mouth, they pray silently the words of the repentant tax collector in Jesus' parable: 'Lord Jesus Christ, have mercy on me, a sinner' (see Lk 18:13). Some will even match their breathing and praying to their heartbeat."

"I like that," she said. "It sounds peaceful."

"It is, but Christians are called to have discernment in such things. There is no reason Christians cannot use yoga as a way of relaxing muscles and seeking inner peace. But they must beware lest the poses they adopt open them to spiritual forces. I don't mean to offend you in saying this, Elaine, but some of the mantras used in transcendental meditation are the names of Hindu deities."

"I am not offended," she graciously replied. "In both Hinduism and Buddhism, we recognize demonic-like creatures that should not be meddled with."

"Exactly! The secular West acts as if we live in what Charles Taylor has called a buffered world, one in which we need not fear the intrusion or interference of supernatural forces that defy our materialistic categories."

"Yes," said Sita with some hesitation in her voice, "but why does it seem that so many Christians want to empty the world of all its magic and mystery?"

"Excellent question," I replied, my face glowing again with professorial pride in the wisdom and sensitivity of my former students, "the answer to which is that the Bible and Christianity do not call for the eradication of magic and mystery."

"I'm glad to hear that," said Sita, "but most Christians I've met are suspicious of such things."

"Some of them are right to be cautious and skeptical. Evil spiritual forces are real, and we must show prudence and discernment. But that does not mean we should throw out magic and fantasy altogether. Though not all Christians would agree with me on this, I think it is helpful and valid to make a distinction between white and black magic."

"What is the difference?" asked Sita.

"White magic," I replied, "seeks a restored sympathy and connection with nature. Black magic seeks power and domination and is willing to pluck forbidden fruit to get it."

"What kind of forbidden fruit?"

"Well, Sita, I'm thinking of those who lust after knowledge we were not meant to possess. It is not good for us to tear down the wall that separates the present from the future or the living from the dead. At the end of his life, King Saul, in utter despair, committed a grave sin by visiting a medium that he hoped would connect him with the ghost of the prophet Samuel (1 Sam 28)."

"Yes," said David, "the Witch of Endor. It seems to me that the witch was mostly a fake, but Samuel showed up anyway and prophesied the coming death of Saul."

"That's right! Saul's search for forbidden wisdom did not end well. Of course, those who seek such wisdom are ultimately seeking power. People who turn to satanism think it will give them control over others; instead, it steals their joy and freedom. Hey, Alex and Stacey, what do I always say about people in movies who serve the villain?"

"Never work for the bad guys!" they chimed in together.

"You remember well!" I said. "In his parable of the good shepherd, Jesus says, 'The thief comes only to steal and kill and destroy. I came that they may have life and have it abundantly' (Jn 10:10). Evil forces may promise us power, pleasure, and influence, but they steal our soul in the end, robbing us of our God-given humanity."

"I agree," said Sita, "but how is that different from white magic?"

"David," I said, "do you remember my *Lord of the Rings* class?"

"How could I forget? That was one of my favorites."

"Thanks! I never get tired of teaching it. Do you remember how we discussed the two kinds of magic that Tolkien includes in his epic?"

"Yes, you called them instrumental magic and sympathetic magic."

"That's right! The first is seen when Saruman tears out the ancient trees of Fangorn forest to fuel his dark, forbidden nurseries, where he so twists and perverts the course of nature as to breed a new and fiercer Orc that can walk in the daylight."

"Yes. Treebeard, the guardian of Fangorn, says that Saruman has a mind of metal and wheels and that he does not care for things that grow."

"You have a good memory, David! All Saruman does works against God's good design for nature and humanity. He is mad for power and control. How different are the elves, who work *with* God's good design."

"Are you thinking of the invisibility cloaks?"

"I am. The cloaks the elves make for the Fellowship do not give them the power to overrule nature. Rather, because the elves have woven into the cloaks the lore of wood and river and stone, the cloaks allow the Fellowship to blend in with the natural world around them."

"Just like a chameleon," said Sita, "but what do invisibility cloaks have to do with white magic?"

"The elves understand the nature of the world God has made, and they work in cooperation with it. You might call them holistic weavers who use their skills to allow the same patterns of energy, the same chi, that runs through nature to run through the cloaks. There is no domination here, no lust for power and control. For the elves, making those cloaks is a form of worship."

"What a lovely image," said Sita with enthusiasm in her voice.

"I think so too. Christianity need not cut us off from the natural world. As long as we do not worship nature herself, as long as we recognize that nature is not our mother but our elder, equally fallen sister, we can learn to live lives of greater harmony and balance. God created us to be stewards of nature. We *are* to rule over her, not to allow her to rule over us, but we are to do so by tending and caring for her (Gen 1:28)."

"Dad," said Stacey, "are you saying again what you always taught us? That the world is full of magic, but we have to have eyes to see it and ears to hear it?"

"Yes, I am. But now I'm thinking less about desire and more about the great magic that stands at the very center of Christianity."

"What's that?" said Bill, who had been trying to follow my rather meandering answer to his original question about New Age spirituality.

"The incarnation, the belief that Jesus was fully God and fully man. There is no greater magic in the world than that. The God who has always been—who knows no boundaries of time or space, for he created both—enters time and space and becomes a man. And yet, in becoming a man, he does not cease to be the eternal, all-present God. I repeat, there is no greater magic than that. If it is true, then we are not alone; our Creator has not forsaken us but has come to us.

"In Hebrew," I said, after pausing to collect my thoughts, "*Jesus* means 'savior,' but Jesus is given another name in the prophecy of the virgin birth. Does anyone know what that name is?"

"'Behold,'" recited David, "'the virgin shall conceive and bear a son, and shall call his name Immanuel' (Is 7:14)."

"Yes, and what does *Immanuel* mean?"

"'God with us.'"

"That is the real magic, my friends, that God has come to us. We in our sinful, mortal state could not go to him, so he came to us. Does anyone remember how we began our discussion before the turkey arrived?"

"Round yon Virgin Mother and child," said Anthony quietly, with a look of wonder in his eyes. "Holy infant so tender and mild."

"The virgin birth is more than a miracle. It was the gateway through which God came to us. And that is something for which we can all be truly thankful!"

FOURTH COURSE

AFTER DINNER BY THE FIRE

11

IS GOD REALLY INVOLVED IN THE WORLD?

UPON COMPLETING MY TWENTY-FIFTH YEAR as an English professor at Houston Christian University, I was invited to choose from a select number of gifts in celebration of my quarter century of service. Rather than choose a fancy clock or bowl or piece of jewelry, I chose a cast-iron fire pit. That may sound like an odd choice, but there are few things I love more than sitting around a fire with friends and family and talking about life.

There's something about a fire that appeals to all the senses at once: the living, breathing glow that moves and stabs with each gust of wind; the gentle fairy sounds of crackling wood and sputtering embers; the intense, focused heat that makes the flesh feel singed without actually burning it; the acrid yet fragrant smell that leaves a bitter but pleasing taste on the tongue. By engaging all five senses in an almost sacramental fashion, the shared fire opens the hearts and minds and tongues of all who draw near it.

Although I am incapable of starting a fire with two matches, much less two pieces of wood, I hoped that by choosing the fire pit, I might be able, with assistance from my Eagle Scout son, to recreate some authentic fire magic in my own backyard. True, the city where I live is not the kind of place where one normally desires to sit outside by a fire; and yet, the occasional cool evening *does* come, even in that nine-month-a-year steam room called Houston.

"Alex," I said, "can you guess what I'm thinking?"

"I haven't the foggiest, Dad."

"I was thinking it's the perfect night to try out the new fire pit. Are you game?"

"Great idea! It's about time we used that thing. It's been sitting in the garage for six months, along with the wood you bought back in September! Come on, Stacey, let's see if we can get it started."

"But it's cold outside."

"It won't be when we get the fire started!"

"All right," said Stacey, with some reluctance in her voice.

"Thank you, kids. All those years of camping with the Scouts were not in vain!"

As my adventurous children put on their coats and headed out to the garage, I turned to the rest of the guests: "Alex and Stacey have gone outside to prepare a treat for us all. Rather than end our Thanksgiving around the piano, we will be ending it around a roaring fire. I hope you're all in the mood for roasting some marshmallows."

One after the other, all the guest nodded their heads—all except one.

"Louis," said Stewart, "I'd love to join you all by the fire, but my bedtime is fast approaching! I leave the late nights to Ali. Still, before I leave, I would like to add my two cents to the evening."

"Please do," I said. "The microphone is yours."

"Well, I've fought in World War II, built a business, helped found a university, raised a family, and traveled around the world, and I can tell you from experience that God is in control. Have I told you the story about Billy Graham?"

"You did, but please share it with the rest of us."

"After many years of hard work, and after putting up our savings for collateral, we finally got Houston Christian off the ground. We would be welcoming our first class in the fall, but I still felt we needed to work harder to get our name out across Houston. So I contacted the superintendent of schools in Houston and asked him whether he would let his high school seniors out early to attend our grand opening ceremonies. He smiled and said he didn't think he could do that."

"So what did you say, Stewart?"

"I made him a proposition. I asked him if he would let the students out if I could get a major public figure, someone like Billy Graham, to speak for the ceremony."

"What did he say to that?"

"He promised that if I could get Billy Graham to speak, he would let his seniors out to hear him. So I went out and got Billy Graham, and the superintendent kept his promise. The first official prayer said over Houston Christian was by Billy Graham himself. As they say, the Lord works in mysterious ways."

"That's one of my favorite HCU stories, but why do you bring it up now?"

"To show that God still performs miracles. It seems like there are a growing number of professors in the universities and seminaries who treat God as if he were distant and removed, uninvolved in the world and in our lives."

"I must sadly agree with you on that, Stewart. What you just described is not true biblical Christianity but deism: the belief that God is a sort of cosmic watchmaker who wound up the universe at the beginning and then stepped back, allowing it to run on its own in accordance with natural laws. I too have met many people who claim to be Christian but who act as if God either can't or won't intervene in human affairs. Strangely enough, I've met more than a few Christians who, though they say they believe each and every miracle recorded in the Bible, are immediately skeptical when they hear a report of God working a miracle today."

"Yes, that's exactly what I mean. Why the reluctance to see the hand of God working directly in natural and human affairs?"

"Stewart, you have raised an excellent topic for conversation around the fire. Though we spoke of miracles before dinner, it is well worth digging behind the scientific issue of miracles to look at the deeper human issue: the doubt so many of us struggle with as to whether God is really concerned, on a personal level, with our individual lives. I'm just sad you won't be able to join us."

"The clock is ticking, and the bed is calling. But I'm glad I was able to initiate what I hope proves to be an engaging topic of conversation. Just don't let Ali give you any trouble!"

"I'll do my best to keep an eye on him! But before you go, let me at least leave you with an exciting piece of news. Something wonderful happened recently that offers decisive proof to all Americans that God still works miracles."

"I'm afraid I don't know what you are referring to. What miracle?"

"The Houston Astros won the World Series! If that's not clear proof of divine intervention, I don't know what is."

The reaction to my proof was mixed indeed, with some guests smiling and nodding, others glaring, and yet others lifting various objects to throw at my head. As for Stewart, he let out a hearty laugh and then used the moment of confusion to slip out the front door. His ninety-eight years had taught him to always have an exit strategy.

When the furor died down and I was able to dodge all missiles hurled at me, I raised up my right arm like a Roman orator and declared that our Thanksgiving celebration was now ready to move outside.

True to his Eagle Scout credentials, Alex had managed to coax a cheerful fire out of the new pit. Stacey, meanwhile, had wiped down the deck chairs and arranged them in a circle around the fire. As for me, I located a bag of marshmallows I had been saving for the last four months and carried it outside, together with a basket full of napkins and a dozen long forks.

While the fire cracked and sputtered, the guests slowly arranged themselves on the seats. They were all wearing jackets when they sat down, but within three minutes, all of them had been removed and draped over the backs of the chairs. As lovely patterns of light and shadow played across their entranced faces, the guests attached marshmallows to their forks and held them out over the pit. The fire was working its subtle, silent magic. All of us had been transformed by its glow into those wide-eyed children that Jesus said we had to become if we wanted to enter the kingdom of God (Mk 10:15).

"Tell me," I said, after biting into my well-charred marshmallow, "has anyone here ever wondered whether God is an absentee landlord, someone who expects his rent every month but never bothers to visit his tenants? Pease don't be afraid to speak up. We're all friends here."

After a long pause, Bill, whom I could always count on to be honest and ask the tough questions, leaned forward and spoke: "I guess I'll start us off. The Bible's full of stories of God talking to people, but where's the evidence he does so today? How *could* he communicate with us in any case? If God is really outside time and space, then it would seem to me to be impossible for that communication to take place."

"That's a good point, Bill. I think it's helpful to remember that heaven is not so much 'up there' as it is alongside us in another dimension. Yes, it's outside our space-time continuum, but it's always breaking through."

"That's a compelling image, but there still seems to me to be a serious disconnect. Real communication should not be possible between two such realms, much less between an eternal, immaterial, transdimensional God and creatures like us."

"You're right, Bill, it shouldn't be. That is why the doctrine of the Trinity is absolutely central to Christianity. Some theologians act as if the Trinity were not essential to the core of Christianity, or, worse, that it were some kind of pagan add-on to the original faith. It is neither. The Trinity, far from being an esoteric doctrine, is a statement about the nature of reality itself."

"What do you mean by that?"

"I mean that the eternal God who created the universe out of nothing has always been capable of being known and being communicated. The First Person of the Trinity, God the Father, is indeed invisible and unknowable, but the Second Person, God the Son, has always been the full expression of the Father, and the Third Person, God the Holy Spirit, has always had the ability to indwell and empower."

"Can you give me an example or analogy of what you're saying?"

"Although there is no human-earthly analogy that can capture the full mystery of the Trinity, the one that comes closest is the analogy of the sun. We never actually see the sun, only the light from the sun. Well, God the Father is like the sun itself, removed from human perception, while God the Son is like the light from the sun, which allows us to see what would otherwise be invisible to our mortal eyes. As for the Holy Spirit, he is like the heat from the sun that warms and quickens into life all it touches and penetrates. We can see and know God the Father, not directly but through the ministry of the Second and Third Persons of the Trinity: We see his glory and his radiance in Jesus, even as we are indwelled by the Holy Spirit."

"That might be true for the New Testament, but what about the Old Testament?"

"Even before God the Son was incarnated into the world as Jesus of Nazareth, he fulfilled the function of revealer of God the Father. When Adam and Eve hear the voice of the Lord God in the garden in the cool of the day (Gen 3:8), or Jacob wrestles with an angelic being (Gen 32:24), or Moses sees the burning bush (Ex 3:2), we seem to be dealing with God the Son in a pre-incarnate form."

"Are you sure of that?"

"To be honest, there is room for scholarly debate on some of those examples, but there are at least two examples in the Old Testament that clearly offer a pre-incarnate appearance of the Second Person of the Trinity. Do you remember the story of the three faithful Jews who were thrown into the fiery furnace by Nebuchadnezzar?"

"Do you mean Meshach, Shadrach, and Abednego?"

"Yes, you remember your Bible stories well! After the three are thrown in the fire for refusing to worship the Babylonian idol, Nebuchadnezzar looks into the furnace and sees not three but four men walking around, and one of them, he exclaims, looks like a son of the gods (Dan 3:25). Certainly this is God the Son in pre-incarnate form protecting and saving the three young men so that they do not even smell of the fire."

"That sounds reasonable. What's the other example?"

"When Jacob flees from his brother Esau after stealing his birthright, he has a dream in which he sees a ladder stretching from earth to heaven and on it the angels of God ascending and descending (Gen 28:12)."

"Yes, I remember that story as well. But what does Jacob's ladder have to do with the Second Person of the Trinity?"

"In John 1, Jesus meets Nathanael and proclaims him a true Israelite in whom there is no guile. When Nathanael asks Jesus how he knows him, he says that he was with him while he was sitting under the fig tree. Amazed that Jesus should know this, Nathanael proclaims him to be the King of Israel and the Son of God. In response, Jesus says: 'Truly, truly, I say to you, you will see heaven opened, and the angels of God ascending and descending on the Son of Man' (Jn 1:51).

"Do you see what Jesus is saying here? He is identifying himself directly with Jacob's ladder. For he *is* Jacob's ladder, the bridge that connects God to man. Jesus is the part of God that interfaces with man, and since God the Son is an eternal member of the Trinity, God has always, even before he created us, been a God who reveals himself to and connects himself with his creatures."

"That is intriguing! But what about the Holy Spirit?"

"Although the permanent indwelling of the Spirit began only after Christ rose and the Spirit descended on the disciples at Pentecost, there are numerous places in the Old Testament where the Spirit temporarily fills and inspires a warrior like Samson (Judg 15:14), a king like David (1 Sam 16:13), or a prophet like Isaiah (Is 61:1). Indeed, whenever the Word of God is spoken by priest, king, or prophet, it is done so through the inspiration of the Holy Spirit. God is not, as he is sometimes depicted to be, a lonely tribal deity thundering on the mountain. God's essence has always included the ability and the desire to be known and communicated.

"In fact, the Bible itself may best be described as a chronicle or record of God's actions and interactions in human history. God does not ignore his creation but reaches out to it continually. When I asked earlier whether God sometimes seems like an absentee landlord, it was because I had Jesus' parable of the tenants in mind."

"I don't recall that one offhand."

"It's not as well-known as the prodigal son or the good Samaritan, but it does offer great insight into the heart—and the wrath—of God. In the parable (Mt 21:33-46), a landowner plants a vineyard and hires tenants to work it for him. When harvest time comes, he sends a servant to collect the rent, but the wicked tenants seize him and kill him. The master then sends several more servants, but the tenants treat them in the same manner. Finally, the master sends his own son, reasoning that they will surely respect his son. But the tenants seize him as well, drag him out of the vineyard, and put him to death. In the end, the master is forced to throw out the wicked tenants and give the vineyard to others."

"That's a pretty stark parable."

"It is. Jesus means it in part to be a summation of the Bible, with the tenants being Israel, the servants being the many lawgivers, judges, priests, and prophets God sent to restore the allegiance of his people, and the son being Jesus, whom the leaders of Israel condemned to death. The passing of the vineyard to new tenants foreshadows the passing of God's covenant relationship from that with Israel to that with the church."

"That's a fascinating parable, but why do you mention it now?"

"Because, Bill, it reminds us that the problem is not so much that God is silent as that we don't want to listen. God has made us all stewards of the gifts and opportunities he has given us, but we, like the bad tenants, prefer to hoard those gifts for ourselves. None of us really wants to feel accountable to our Creator for what he has given us. And yet, despite our stubbornness, God keeps reaching out to us: through the Bible, through circumstances, through other people, through our conscience. He never ceases speaking and reaching out, but we just won't have ears to hear. In fact, according to Jesus himself, the reason he preached in parables was so that only those with ears to hear would hear."

"I thought he taught in parables because they were simple and could be easily understood by everyone."

"That's what I used to think as well. It's certainly what I was taught in Sunday school. But that's not what Jesus says when the disciples ask him to interpret the parable of the sower. Before offering the interpretation, Jesus says this: 'To you has been given the secret of the kingdom of God, but for those outside everything is in parables, so that "they may indeed see but not perceive, and may indeed hear but not understand, lest they should turn and be forgiven"' (Mk 4:11-12)."

"Didn't we discuss this before dinner?"

"You have a good memory! I mentioned this teaching of Jesus briefly when Anthony asked whether miracles broke the laws of nature. I argued then that miracles are like the deeper meanings and patterns hidden beneath the surface of Shakespeare's plays; we will miss both unless we have eyes that are willing to search for and to see that deeper weave. Well, the same goes for the voice of God. God may speak to us in three or four different ways, but if we don't want to hear what he is saying, we won't."

"Why doesn't God speak louder?"

"Think of the sun shining down brightly on a piece of wax and a pot of mud. Though the rays that strike the wax and the mud are the same, they will likely have a very different impact on the two materials. While the wax turns soft and pliable, the mud turns hard and brittle. So it is with the Word of God, in whatever form it reaches us. If we receive it like the wax, it will work in our hearts to make us more obedient and grateful. But if we receive it like the mud, we will become resistant and stiff-necked, made bitter by the very thing that would do us good.

"Please forgive me if I'm sounding a bit preachy here. The fact is that we all possess some mud and some wax in our souls. On our good days, when all is going well, we are open to a word from above, even if that word is not what we had hoped to hear. But when we are angry or resentful or have done or said things that we know are hurtful and wrong, then we resist quite fiercely any message from above that would force us to examine ourselves. Sometimes we are in between the wax and the mud: listening intently for God's voice but willing to hear it only if it comes in the way we expect."

I intended to follow that last sentence with an illustration, but I found myself suddenly bereft of one. Luckily, God came through just in time.

"Dr. Markos," said David, when he noticed my frustrated face, "why don't you tell the story about the drowning man?"

"Thanks, David, that's a great idea. There once was a man whose boat capsized, leaving him bobbing up and down in the waves. The man is a Christian, and so he prays to God to save him. A few minutes later, a boat sails by and calls on the man to come aboard. But he shoos the boat away, for he is waiting for God to answer his prayer. A few minutes after that, a helicopter appears above him and lets down a ladder. But, again, the man rejects the ladder, for he prefers to wait for God to answer him.

"Eventually, the man drowns, and his soul ascends to heaven. Saint Peter comes out to greet him, but the man does not speak to him at first. Peter asks him what is wrong, and the man says, somewhat indignantly, that he is still upset that God did not answer his prayer. 'Not answer your prayer,' says Peter with a shocked expression. 'Who do you think sent the boat and the helicopter!'"

As I finished telling the story, David threw a handful of leaves into the fire pit, causing it to flare up in a burst of white gold.

"Thanks, David," I said, "for supplying that great exclamation point! Even when we say we are willing to heed God's voice, we don't always mean it. I remember once that a gifted woman prayed over me during a time I was seeking God's direction. As she prayed over me, God gave her a vision of a soldier following after a fast-moving general. The soldier kept crying out to the general to stop and give him his orders. Finally, the general stopped, faced the soldier, and placed his two hands firmly on the eager GI's shoulders. The general then turned the soldier around with a swift jerk of his hands and told him to march in the other direction."

"Hey, Dad," said Alex, "I think that was God's way of preparing you to leave Michigan and move to Texas."

"I think you're right, Alex! I was open to go to whatever school God sent me, but I never thought in a million years he would send a Yankee like me down to Houston. Thankfully, I trusted and obeyed him that time, and as a result I have spent a quarter of a century working for a university I love and that has loved me in return—a university, I might add, that has allowed me to exercise every gift God has given me and to use every bit of knowledge and experience he has taught me over the years."

"You know, Dad, God did something quite similar to me when it came to what college I would attend."

"Please share the story with us, Alex."

"Well, all my life, I had dreamed about attending Houston Christian. I had visited the university hundreds of times, had sat in classes, gone to school functions, and even played in the pep band. I did look seriously at two other colleges in Michigan, Hillsdale and Hope, but when it came down to it, I accepted HCU's offer. When I did that, I felt greatly relieved . . . at least for the next twenty-four hours.

"You see, even when I accepted HCU, I knew I wasn't supposed to go there. A week earlier, God had spoken to me—not with words but through a divine presence that shook me to the core—that he wanted me to go to Hope. But that wasn't what I wanted to do; it went against all my plans of attending HCU. God, as it turned out, wasn't going to let me get away so easily. Shortly after I accepted Houston Christian, I was taking a shower when the Holy Spirit assaulted me. 'I told you that you were supposed to go to Hope,' he said, shaking me once again to the very soles of my feet. I knew my dad wasn't going to be happy, but I had to tell him what God had told me. You were pretty upset, Dad, weren't you?"

"I must admit that I was. But then you and I, Alex, spent the entire weekend praying intensely that God would find a way to make his will clear to both of us at once. And he did! That Sunday, our pastor preached on John 21: That's the chapter where Peter the fisherman, even though he has seen the risen Christ, returns to his nets and his boats. But Jesus calls him a second time to leave his old life behind and follow him. As it turns out, I had written a short story about that very incident when I was Alex's age. I read the story out loud to Alex, and we were both reduced to tears. From that moment, we both knew that it was God's will that Alex go to Hope."

"Did you ever doubt that in the coming months?" asked Bill.

"I can honestly say that I never doubted for a moment and still don't doubt today that God wanted Alex at Hope. Alex and I stayed in close contact throughout his years at Hope, discussing his classwork and all his extracurricular activities. It was hard for both of us, but God grew Alex in tremendous ways while he was there, matching him with some excellent professors and allowing him to spend a semester studying in Athens, Greece.

"By the way, there is an addendum to this happy-ending story in which God spoke and Alex and I listened, even though listening disrupted both our plans. In two months, Alex will begin an online master's program in apologetics at HCU! As he continues to teach in Boerne, he will be taking classes with HCU's premier apologetics professors."

"Dad," said Stacey with a mischievous smile, "don't forgot to tell everyone that I'll be graduating from HCU in May with a degree in vocal performance. To quote our pastor, I was the 'good child' who stayed in Houston!"

"Sorry, Alex, I'm afraid your sister has you there. Still, if you would like to throw some marshmallows at her, you can do so now!"

Stacey quickly ducked, but she didn't have to. The spirit of Thanksgiving had settled in, and Alex spared her any sticky missiles. Instead, he grabbed a handful of leaves and tossed them in the fire, producing another flash of white and gold.

"My friends," I said, gazing at the faces illuminated by the fiery blaze, "we've all struggled in our own way with the seeming silence of God. But he is not silent, and he has not forgotten us. He moves and he guides. You've all met David's parents, Bobby and Martha, though Martha, true to her biblical namesake (Lk 10:38-42), has been so busy working in the kitchen that some of you haven't had a chance to visit with her. Who could've guessed that a boy from India and a girl from Mexico would come to America, meet each other, marry, have David and his sister Esther, and start the Houston International Christian Fellowship? The Thanksgiving potluck we are enjoying today is a ministry of that fellowship.

"You can call the meeting of Bobby and Martha a coincidence, but the fruit it has borne pays tribute to God's hand at work. Tell us, Bobby, has this fellowship always run smoothly?"

"Hardly," said Bobby. "We've gone through many ups and downs over the last thirty years. But we've also seen lives changed, marriages formed, and people from all over the world edified and encouraged. For a while, the fellowship even functioned as its own church, but then God later took us in a different direction."

"And isn't it true, Bobby, that the fellowship almost ended a few years back?"

"Oh, I'm sure you could have kept it going yourself."

"No, no, I'm a good host and a seasoned Bible study leader, but you and Martha, and now David too, are the glue that holds it all together. But tell us what happened."

"Well, I work for Exxon up in the Woodlands, and with the recession and other changes, I came very close to being moved to our offices in Dallas."

"Had Bobby's family moved to Dallas," I said, casting my eye around the circle, "that would have marked the end of the fellowship. But that didn't happen, did it?"

"No, Lou, God opened a door and moved me to another division. For the last four or five years, I've been spearheading a very large project in Romania. It has meant lots of trips overseas, but it has allowed us to stay in Houston."

"Friends," I said, "we may be nothing more than statistics to the big governments and big businesses of the world, but we are each a unique individual in the eyes of the God who created us. God speaks all the time, but the world in which we live is so full of noise and stress and anxiety that it's a wonder we can ever hear his voice rising above the incessant din. But times of silence and meditation do come, even to our busy, hectic lives. It's then that we must listen."

"But, if I may," said Anthony, who had been staring into the fire for some time, "it's not just the noise and business that drown out his voice. It's the pain and the suffering that assaults us at every turn that makes God seem distant and uncaring."

"Anthony, you have raised what is surely the most difficult question of all, what theologians and philosophers call the problem of pain. I think the time has come for us to face that issue head-on. But now that we are out here by the fire and have let down our hair, I would like to address the problem of pain not in an abstract, logical kind of way but in a more personal, intimate way. I would also like to discuss it in terms of the international nature of our gathering. Does that sound all right with you, Anthony?

"Yes, I'd prefer that."

"Good. Then let us begin."

12

WHY DO BAD THINGS HAPPEN TO GOOD PEOPLE?

"**ANY DISCUSSION OF THE PROBLEM OF PAIN**," I said, "must begin with a simple truth that is too often overlooked. Pain and suffering are not a problem unless you believe, as the Bible teaches, that God is all-powerful and all-loving."

"You're going to have to explain that one," said Anthony.

"Well, Anthony, if someone is a pure Darwinist—that is to say, if he believes that all we see is the result of natural selection—should he be upset or even surprised by the great amount of pain and suffering in the world?"

"Hmm, I see what you mean. If Darwin is right, then pain and suffering are the very mechanisms by which evolution operates. There can be no evolution unless the weaker species dies out and the stronger survives."

"Exactly. Now let me quickly add that Darwinists are not, as a group, cold and unfeeling people. They show great compassion for those who are ill and dying, but when they show that compassion, they are not being consistent with what they say they believe about the nature of the world. They also, thankfully, reveal themselves as inconsistent when they fight against injustice. There can be no ultimate justice or injustice in a purely Darwinian world, for there can be no standard to measure it by. Natural selection, as you just said, means a world in which the strong survive and the weak die out. Anthony, did they teach you in your biology classes what the subtitle to Darwin's *Origin of Species* is?"

"I believe the full title is *On the Origin of Species by Means of Natural Selection*."

"That's correct, but there's a second part to the title."

"I don't remember being taught that."

"I'm not surprised. The subtitle is more often than not airbrushed out. Here's the full title: *On the Origin of Species by Means of Natural Selection, or the Preservation of Favoured Races in the Struggle for Life*. The subtitle is usually left out because it stands as a reminder of the direct link between Darwinism and eugenics. Totalitarian nations from the right and the left have been practicing their own versions of Darwinian genocide for the last hundred years. In our own country, Darwinian eugenicists even advocated for forced sterilization of undesirable people."

"That was certainly a dark period in our history."

"It was, Anthony, but the only reason we are bothered by it or consider it unjust is that most people, whatever they *say* they believe, find natural selection unjust and morally repellent. But that is decidedly odd, is it not? If we are merely the product of natural selection, how is it that we find that process both offensive and wrong?

"Actually, if I may hark back to something we discussed during dessert, one might call natural selection a perversion of the chosenness of the Jews. Yes, God did set aside the Jews as a favored nation, but he did that so the Jews could be a blessing to all the other nations. As I admitted, the Jews rarely lived up to that high calling, and that's why God punished them and sent them into exile. With survival of the fittest, however, it is to be expected that favored races will destroy weaker ones. If Darwin is right, that is the nature of the world, and we shouldn't make such a big fuss about it."

"That's a tough thing to say, but I think it's justified. If the gazelle could speak as it was being devoured by the lion, I don't think it would say, 'How unjust the world is.' It would just die in accordance with the laws of the jungle."

"That's right, Anthony. Our sense of justice points to a standard higher than natural selection. In fact, it points to a loving God who is also the architect of right and wrong."

"If I may ask, Dr. Markos," said Sita, "why does that God have to be the God of the Bible? Can't he be any God of any religion?"

"Back when the lights went out, Sita, I argued that the pagan nations were given glimpses of truth by way of general revelation. Although those glimpses allowed them to see something of God's glory and goodness, the pagan religions of Greece and Rome were founded on gods who were not so much cruel as arbitrary.

"The only religious consolation Achilles is able to find in the last book of the *Iliad* is to say that Zeus has two jars before his throne, one filled with blessings and the other with curses. When Zeus pours out the contents of the former, all goes well with us, but when he pours out the latter, life is filled with pain and suffering. But Achilles gives no hope that the choices of Zeus are guided by any kind of standard or even by a sense of love and compassion. That is why there is no real problem of pain in the pagan world. It arises only when the writer catches a glimpse of a higher type of justice, as happens occasionally in Greek tragedy and much more often in Plato and Aristotle."

"That makes sense, but what about Hinduism?"

"Sita, the Indians are a kind and hospitable people, but until recently, little was done to alleviate the pain and suffering of those in the lower castes. Why do you think that is?"

"I'm not sure."

"What do you think, Bobby?"

"I think it's because of the Hindu doctrine of karma. According to the laws of karma, if a poor person suffers, it is because of sins he committed in his previous life."

"Bobby, I agree with you. Hinduism is not haunted by the problem of pain in the way Christianity is because karma takes care of the problem. Yes, the Hindu gods tend to be as capricious as those of Greece and Rome, but karma points to a divine, if impersonal, system of merits and demerits that meets out punishments and rewards.

"To put this in perspective, there was one church father named Origen who tried to deal with the unfairness of some people being born rich and others poor, some healthy and other sickly, by suggesting that our status on earth is determined by actions we committed in the period when our souls preexisted in heaven. Needless to say, his theories in this regard were rejected by all the church fathers."

"Weren't there Jews in Jesus' day who also took a karmic approach to suffering?"

"There were, Bobby, but Jesus clearly denied this view. When he came upon a blind man and the disciples asked him whether his blindness was the result of his sins or his father's sins, Jesus answered, 'It was not that this man sinned, or his parents, but that the works of God might be displayed in him' (Jn 9:3). If the universe were really run by some cosmic principle of karma, then pain and suffering would not be a problem."

"What about Buddhism?" asked Elaine.

"As you know, Elaine, most forms of Buddhism also rely on a karmic system of merits and demerits. But there is a deeper aspect of Buddhism that ultimately renders the problem of pain a nonissue. Buddhism looks on the world as *maya*, or illusion. Pain is a problem only because we think it is one. When we reach enlightenment, we rise above such things.

"Incidentally, this Buddhist concept has also had an advocate in the West in the person of Mary Baker Eddy, founder of Christian Science. For Eddy, pain and disease are finally illusions we must learn to see through. Her form of spiritual healing may seem to resemble that of Jesus, but it is based on a completely different worldview. Jesus accepted the full reality of pain, suffering, and illness but then performed miracles to stem, temporarily, the decay inherent in our fallen world. Eddy believed that that decay is an illusion and that we can therefore find healing by simply convincing ourselves we are healthy."

"Well," said Reza, "I suppose that leaves Islam. Surely pain and suffering are problems in Islam since the Qur'an describes God as all-powerful and all-merciful."

"Yes, Reza, the problem of pain does surface in Islam as it does in Judaism. And yet, I would argue that only Christianity offers the necessary resources for dealing with the problem."

"What resources are those?"

"The Christian doctrines of the fall and the cross."

"You're going to need to explain that in much greater detail!"

Knowing that I would need all my wits about me to explain the Christian understanding of the fall of man and the crucifixion of Christ, I paused long enough to pop another well-done marshmallow in my mouth. The surge of sugar gave me the energy I needed to proceed.

"Although both the Old Testament (Gen 3) and the Qur'an (7:10-27) tell the story of the fall of Adam and Eve, neither religion develops that event into the full Christian doctrine of original sin. Judaism and Islam recognize that we are people who sin and rebel and disobey, but only Christianity teaches that we are sinners. Only in the fuller revelation of the New Testament is it made clear that we, as fallen people, possess a sinful nature that prevents us from saving ourselves by good actions alone."

"From what I know about Judaism and Islam, that seems like a fair statement, but what does it have to do with the problem of pain?"

"Reza, we can't understand the full causes and functions of pain and suffering until we realize that we and our world have been broken and subjected to entropy and decay by Adam and Eve's freewill choice to disobey God and eat the forbidden fruit."

"That's a mouthful," said Reza, and then quickly added, "No pun intended!"

"It is indeed. In the biblical reckoning, survival of the fittest is not the mechanism by which we were fashioned but a result of the fall. It is because of sin that we live in a world where nature is, to quote Alfred Lord Tennyson, 'red in tooth and claw.' The world is not now as God created it to be in the beginning. God said of that world that it was good (Gen 1:10, 12, 18, 21, 25) and of us, the creatures he made to steward it, that it was very good (Gen 1:31). Now, however, nature shows the ravages of sin, even as we ourselves bear the marks of the fall.

"Because of the fall, wrote Paul, 'the creation was subjected to futility' (Rom 8:20) and longs to be 'be set free from its bondage to corruption and obtain the freedom of the glory of the children of God' (Rom 8:21). Indeed, 'the whole creation has been groaning together in the pains of childbirth until now. And not only the creation, but we ourselves, who have the firstfruits of the Spirit, groan inwardly as we wait eagerly for adoption as sons, the redemption of our bodies' (Rom 8:22-23)."

"Wow, those are beautiful verses!"

"They are, Anthony—beautiful because they remind us that the death, decay, and disease we see all around us, both in ourselves and in nature, are temporary and will someday give way to a state of true freedom and incorruptibility. But until that glorious day arrives, we must live out our lives in a broken, fragmented world. Anthony, did you ever notice how people continually complain that the world should be better than it is?"

"Yes, I've noticed that. I've thought and said it myself many times."

"So have I. But why do we say it? The world has never been better than it is. There has always been war and famine and injustice. Yet still we persist in saying it. The only answer that makes sense to me is that we all carry within us a memory of Eden, of that lost paradise that so briefly housed our first parents. By the way, Reza, did you know that *paradise* is an ancient Persian word that means 'walled garden'?"

"I didn't know that, but we Persians do love our gardens; in fact, the Qur'an frequently describes heaven as a garden of delight."

"It does. Blissful gardens with thornless trees, flowing water, abundant fruits, cool drinks that don't cause intoxication or headaches, and modest maidens with beautiful eyes (37:40-49; 56:11-40). Not a bad way to spend eternity!"

"I'll second that," said Reza.

"So we've lost the original garden made for Adam and Eve, and we yearn for that greater garden that awaits us in heaven, but what are we to do during the long, painful road that separates the two? We can't simply go back to Eden or leap forward to heaven, for our sin has cut us off from God and from paradise. To get from the one to the other, we must die to our old life and be reborn and resurrected in Christ. It's a painful process, but that's only because we chose to do it the hard way."

"I, for one," said Bill, "have always thought that the doctrine of original sin was unfair. Why should we be punished for what Adam and Eve did?"

"I can sympathize with that, Bill. But however one understands the workings of original sin, the fact remains that we all commit our own sins.

We all rebel and disobey and insist on doing it our own way. The majority of suffering in the world is caused by human beings driven by pride or greed or envy or lust."

"What about natural disasters?"

"We must remember that nature is fallen as well. The stain of depravity that runs through all of us runs through the natural and animal world as well. I suppose that one could argue that that's unfair, but that's the upshot of nature being subjected to futility. Still, in the midst of all this pain and suffering, we continue to know deep inside that we were made for the garden."

"Why," said Anthony, "do you keep coming back to that point?"

"Because pain and suffering are problems only when we recognize that they are problems, but we can recognize them as such only if we possess, hardwired into the core of our being, a countervision for how the world should really be. If we are merely products of natural selection, then we should never have developed a belief that we were made by a good and loving God. That's not where the hard evidence points. We don't believe in a loving God *because* of the pain we experience but in spite of it."

"You sound like you're arguing against yourself."

"I see why you would say that, Anthony, but what I'm trying to get at is that all our wrestling against pain doesn't come from nature but from something within us that cries out against it. We still manage, miraculously, to see God's hand in our suffering, for we are conscious that God has the power to use it to mold us into the creatures he created us to be, and that he promises we will someday be again, if we will only trust and obey him.

"I don't know whether you've noticed it, Anthony, but the more our modern world succeeds in shielding us from pain, disease, and discomfort, the more we complain about the problem of pain. The Christians of the past had far more to complain about than we do, yet they did not consider the problem of pain to be the great obstacle to faith that it has become today."

"That's a good point and a true one."

"I don't want to sound condescending, Anthony, but most of the modern books that express the greatest outrage against pain and suffering were written by White, healthy, well-off academics. The more entitled we feel, the angrier we seem to get when the world is not the way we think it should be.

Oddly, that anger very often leads people both to hate the God of the Bible and to argue that he does not exist."

"That sounds rather contradictory."

"It is! It's like the friend I mentioned while we were eating dessert who said he hated God and then went on to say that what he really hated about God is that he sends people to hell. In that example, my friend did not understand that heaven means being in the direct presence of God forever. In the case of New Atheists who use pain as a knockout punch against the existence of an all-powerful, all-loving God, the misunderstanding rests on what it means to say that God is powerful and loving."

"What do you mean by that?"

"Many people who use the problem of pain to dismiss Christianity take for granted, whether they realize it or not, that an omnipotent and loving God would always rescue us from pain and suffering."

"Isn't that obvious?"

"At first glance, it might seem so, but not when we study the matter more closely. Our world has been subjected to futility. Just because God is omnipotent doesn't mean he can do whatever he wants. Yes, in the end, the old heaven and the old earth will be destroyed and remade, but until that day, we live in a world in which sin and disease and entropy are endemic. God does perform miracles now and then that temporarily stem or reverse the process of decay, but if God were to do that again and again, I doubt that our world could maintain its integrity."

"But what about his love? Does God not care when he sees us in pain?"

"Parents who truly love their children don't always rescue them from pain. Sometimes the most loving thing a parent can do for a child is to let him suffer: not as an end in itself but as part of a process that will help him to grow into the fuller person he has the potential to be. Too often we limit our view of God's love, treating God as if he were concerned only about our momentary happiness rather than our overall welfare."

"Are you saying God causes pain and suffering to help us grow?"

"Sometimes, perhaps, but more often than not God makes redemptive use of the pain and suffering that are a part of our fallen world. God does not inflict bad; rather, he takes the bad and uses it for good. Indeed, God showed his power and his love most perfectly by taking that most painful and bitter of events, the fall of man, and using it as the vehicle for a greater and more lasting good."

"How did he do that?"

"Stacey, can you tell me the two-word Latin phrase I have in mind?"

"I can. *Felix culpa*. That's one of my favorite phrases!"

"Well done! Can you tell us what it means?"

"It means 'happy guilt,' and it refers to the fall of man."

"Well done again. But how can that guilt be happy?"

"Because it led to the incarnation of Jesus."

"Excellent! God's creation of the world was an act of love. Because God has always existed as a Trinity, he is complete in himself and does not need an outside object either to love him or to be loved by him. Still, out of love, he made a world separate from himself. But that act of love, great as it is, is nothing compared to the love God demonstrated in the incarnation. Though complete in himself, God left heaven and became a mortal man. That cosmic act of love was God's response to the evil of the fall, a response that took the greatest of evils and transformed it into the greatest of goods.

"But tell us, Stacey, are the fall and incarnation the only example of *felix culpa*, or do the Gospels record a second one?"

"They do. When Jesus was crucified on Good Friday, that was a terrible thing, but that terrible thing led to the victory of Easter."

"Stacey, you have passed your oral final exam with flying colors. Have another marshmallow to celebrate!

"Do you all understand what Stacey just shared with us? There could have been no resurrection without the crucifixion. The fathers of the church understood that well; that's why they made the rather strange choice to call the worst day in human history *Good* Friday. Taken alone, the crucifixion was not good, but when we realize what God *did* with that grievous miscarriage of justice, we see that a very bad thing can lead to a very good thing. So it is with the positive things God accomplishes by working through our pain to help us grow and mature."

"Dr. Markos," said Sita, who had been listening very intently, "I understand what you are saying, and I can see that God often brings good out of bad, but what I want to know is whether God really cares. Does God really sympathize with us? For that matter, *can* he sympathize with us? What does he really know of human suffering?"

"To answer that we must turn to the second resource that is unique to Christianity. We have spoken of the fall; let us speak now of the cross.

"When bad things happen to us, it is not enough to know that we will get through the pain. What we really need to know and to be assured of is that God is there and truly sympathizes with us. It is there that the supposed absence and silence of God are felt most deeply and grievously; but it is also there, in that dark place, that the Christian gospel speaks most powerfully."

"In what way?" asked Sita.

"God shows his love when he delivers us from pain. But he shows even greater love when he enters into that pain and suffers alongside us. Ultimately, the answer to the problem of pain is on the cross. When Jesus hung on the cross, he did more than take the penalty for our sins; he identified fully with our pain. When Jesus says to us in our pain that he knows how we feel, he *means* it. He suffered all we suffer and so much more.

"Sita, have you ever heard people before claim that they felt your pain, that they knew and understood exactly what you were going through?"

"Yes, many times."

"Were they telling the truth?"

"Not really. I suppose some of them *thought* they were telling the truth, but I don't think any of them could really understand what I was feeling."

"Why is that?"

"Because they couldn't crawl inside me and see it from my perspective."

"Well put! There are lots of movies out there in which people switch bodies for a day, but they are just fantasies. How can anyone fully empathize with our pains and our sufferings, our struggles and doubts, our anxieties and humiliations? And if another person, even a close friend or family member, can't do that, then how can an eternal, invisible, all-powerful God do it?"

"I'm not sure, but I certainly hope there's a way; otherwise, we're sort of on our own down here."

"If Christianity is true, then God *did* find a way. So great was his desire to know and understand us that he chose to become exactly like us, to wear our skin, to become a human being in the fullest, most radical sense. He left himself no easy outs. All the pains and indignities, all the fevers and fatigues, all the stubbed toes and upset stomachs and pounding headaches: he experienced them all.

"More importantly, Sita, Jesus can understand us fully because he himself was misunderstood. Our loneliness, our frustration, our rage against the system: he suffered them all. When Jesus revealed in the synagogue of Nazareth that he was the Messiah, his own townspeople tried to kill him. They called him a blasphemer and an enemy of Israel (Lk 4:14-30). His family thought he was crazy (Mk 3:21), and his brothers did not believe in him (Jn 7:5). When Jesus was a boy and taught in the temple, the teachers of the law thought he was cute, a spiritual child prodigy (Lk 2:41-50). But when he got older, they saw him only as a threat."

"I think I see what you mean. Maybe God really can understand us. But what about the cross?"

"In suffering the agony of the cross, Jesus experienced the very limits of physical pain, but he did far more than that."

"What could be more than that?"

"Sita, when Christians think about Jesus on the cross, they almost always put all their focus on the pain. Now, don't get me wrong, crucifixion is widely regarded as the most painful way to die. That's why the Romans used it to break the spirits of their enemies. That's also why Roman citizens were exempt from death by crucifixion. But Jesus endured something worse than physical pain."

"What do you mean?"

"Sita, did you know our bodies don't remember pain? You can remember it hurt terribly when you broke your arm at age twelve, but you don't reexperience the pain."

"I think we discussed that in one of my nursing classes."

"Actually, I can give you a simple proof that we don't remember pain. Sita, are you an only child?"

"No, I have a younger brother."

"There you have your proof. If women fully remembered the physical pain of childbirth, very few of us would have younger siblings!"

"That's a good proof!"

"I think it's airtight! But, to get serious again, there is something nobody ever forgets. Let's say that, when you were twelve years old, your father chewed you out and told you that you were worthless. If I were to ask you right now to remember that moment, to call it back to your mind, what do you think would happen?"

"My face would get red, my body would tense up, and I would start to cry."

"Exactly. Our body may not remember physical pain, but it never forgets the deeper, more scarring pain of humiliation, abandonment, and betrayal. When we speak about the problem of pain, what more often causes us to give in to despair is not the physical pain but the feeling of utter abandonment."

"I agree with you, but how does the cross save us from that?"

"If Jesus were here and we could ask him what the worst part of the crucifixion was, I don't think he would say it was the physical pain. I think he would say it was the betrayal of Judas, the denial of Peter, the public humiliation of the trial and scourging, the rejection of his people, the jeering of the crowd, and something even more crushing, terrible, and heart-wrenching."

"What do you mean?"

"While Jesus hung on the cross, he not only took on our sin, but he *became* sin, became a curse. When that happened, his own Father turned his face away, causing Jesus to cry out, 'My God, my God, why have you forsaken me?' (Mt 27:46). I cannot fathom the emotional and spiritual devastation, the utter and absolute isolation that Jesus must have experienced in his final moments on the cross."

"How horrible!"

"Yes, and yet how wonderful to know that the same God who created us can sympathize with us, even when we are in the blackest pit of despair: when we have given up on love, on joy, on hope; when we feel trapped in an uncaring universe in which pain is nothing more than pain. It is in those moments that the one Isaiah called 'a man of sorrows and acquainted with grief' (Is 53:3) invites us to sit and weep together with him."

"Thank you for sharing that. To know that even Jesus himself felt abandoned by God gives me almost as much hope as to know that he rose from the dead."

"As it should give hope to us all. God is a victorious God who defeated Satan, sin, and death. But he is also a close God who was tempted and suffered in every way."

"But, Dr. Markos, if I may be so bold, could you please share with us how God has worked in your life? I've been in your class and heard you teach, and it often seems to your students that you have a perfect life and that you are always happy. Have you ever been scared or hurt or confused, and, if so, how did God minister to you?"

"Sita, I usually keep my personal struggles private, but tonight I'm going to break that rule. Sitting here with you all by the fire, I feel a special peace and intimacy that assures me that it would be a good and proper thing for me to share with you my own struggles and the miraculous ways in which the risen Christ met me in the darkness."

13

HOW HAS GOD WORKED IN *YOUR* LIFE?

AS I STARED ONE BY ONE into the faces around the fire, I realized how special this Thanksgiving had been. In our conversations in the den, around the dinner table, and on the deck, we had ranged from miracles to pain, philosophy to theology, literature to history. We had tackled the big questions of life and had even wrestled, like Jacob, with God himself. But the time had now come to make it more personal, to bare my soul before this wonderfully diverse group of caring people who had gathered at my home from many different nations and different religions.

As David and Alex had already done, I scooped up a pile of leaves and tossed them into the pit. For the third time that evening, the fire exploded in a burst of gold and white, making it seem for a second that the sun had returned overhead.

"I shared earlier how difficult it was for me when God led my son, Alex, away from Houston Christian University to attend college in the cold northern climes of Michigan. And yet, there was a sort of divine symmetry to my son's calling. Twenty-one years earlier, God had called me to leave Michigan for the warm southern wetlands of Houston. The call left me as confused, frightened, and apprehensive as Alex. Why would God send me to Texas?

"My friends, people always talk about how prejudiced the South is against the North, but it has been my experience that the North is far more prejudiced against the South. Growing up in New Jersey and attending universities in New York and Michigan, I had unconsciously absorbed the firm but unquestioned notion that I would never want to live down south. Texas might as well have been the end of the world."

"Then how did you end up here?"

"Because, Sita, the Lord does indeed work in mysterious ways. Like most students in the final year of their PhD program, I sent cover letters and résumés to fifty different colleges and universities across America. If any of the schools I applied to found my letter and résumé interesting, they would write back and ask for a sample of my work. All except HCU, who sent me a long form that had to be filled out on a typewriter: a form that asked for exactly the same information that was already on my résumé.

"Now, you must understand that although I was open to going anywhere God led, I had already decided in my mind that there were three things God would almost certainly not ask me to do: live down south, live in a big city, and work at a Christian university. That meant that Houston Christian University was at the very bottom of my list. When I opened the letter from HCU, it was two o'clock in the morning; I was working away diligently at my dissertation and had neither the time nor the inclination to fill out a complicated form for a school I would never want to teach at. In fact, I vividly remember tossing the letter from HCU into the garbage before turning back to my dissertation."

"What happened next?"

"What happened next is that the Holy Spirit turned my head into a buzzing beehive. When I looked down at the trash, my head would clear, but when I tried to work on my dissertation, the buzzing would start all over again. After enduring this for thirty minutes, I got fed up and went to bed. But the buzzing continued. I could get no relief from it no matter how much I tossed and turned. Finally, I returned to my desk and said to God, 'Okay, I'll fill out the HCU form. I won't go there, but I'll fill out the form.' The very second I finished filling it out, a sense of peace and calm flowed over me. I went back to bed and immediately fell asleep.

"About the same time God forced open the window to HCU, he closed the door on a second Christian school that would have been ideal. I used a pretty standard cover letter for all the schools I applied to, but, when it came to Calvin College in Grand Rapids, Michigan, I tried to insert a short sentence in which I identified myself as an evangelical Christian. When I tried to do that, my word processor went crazy, adding seven or eight lines to my cover letter and messing up all the spaces and indents. It made no sense why the addition of a line would throw everything out of whack that way, but that's exactly what it did. After trying a dozen ways to fix it, I finally gave up and removed the added line. Immediately, everything fixed itself."

"That's a funny story, but what does it have to do with God leading you here?"

"Although I can't prove it, I firmly believe that had I added that sentence, Calvin would have written me back and eventually offered me a job."

"I still don't see the connection."

"Sita, had I been accepted to HCU and Calvin College, it would have been nearly impossible for God to lead me down to Houston. Not only would God have had to appear to me bodily to convince me to choose HCU over Calvin; he would have had to appear to my parents, my wife, and her parents as well. Wild horses couldn't have dragged us away from the safe Calvin to the exotic and unfamiliar HCU. But Houston Christian is where God wanted me, even if it meant stooping to mess with my word processor!"

"Well, I'm certainly glad you chose to come to HCU! But tell me, once you accepted HCU's offer, did you feel at peace?"

"Not at first. Inside I was still in turmoil. My wife and I had no close friends or family within a thousand miles of Houston. I was still filled with uncertainties and fears for the future. Could this really be what God wanted me to do? Would he really be with me in this adventure? I felt like Abraham leaving all that was familiar to venture into a shadowy Promised Land that didn't seem particularly promising. I needed a clear sign from the Lord if I was to begin my new life with confidence and clarity."

"Did you get the sign you prayed for?"

"Yes, but in a way I could never have guessed. While at the University of Michigan, I gave sermons and led Bible studies for a Korean Christian student group on campus. They knew how dearly I loved to worship with them, and so, when I preached my last sermon, they surprised me with a cassette recording of the group singing their favorite hymns and worship songs. Somewhere in the middle of our twelve-hundred-mile journey from Michigan to Texas, I popped in the tape to listen to the songs. As I quietly sang along with the first three, my mind filled with joyful memories of my years with the Korean fellowship.

"And then the fourth song began, a song based on Psalm 91 that I couldn't remember having sung with them before. Not knowing the words, my mind drifted and began to meditate on the long miles that still lay before me . . . and the even longer years. I needed the Lord's clear presence and guidance if I was to weather this difficult transition. That's when my ear picked up on the chorus to the song: 'Blest be the Lord, blest be the Lord / The God of mercy, the God who saves. / I shall not fear the dark of night / Nor the arrow that flies by day.'

"The worshipers on the tape repeated the chorus three times, but to me it seemed as if they sang it over and over again. Then time and space began doing strange things. In a mystical, suspended moment that I can't express fully in human words, time seemed to stand still while I was transported to a meeting of the Korean fellowship. In the wink of an eye, I saw the faces of all the students raptured in praise and discerned a Presence among them whose rough carpenter hands were stretched out toward me.

"Suddenly, I became conscious of a tear welling up in my eye. I turned to my wife and said, 'Look, I'm crying.' The moment I said those words, some kind of floodgate deep inside me opened, and I began to weep uncontrollably. As a Greek, I've never had a problem crying during movies or songs or nostalgic family gatherings, but I had never before experienced weeping on this level. When my wife saw the extent to which my eyes were bathed in tears, her face grew tense with fear—for, you see, I was driving a sixteen-foot Ryder truck with no rear window and our car attached to it on a trailer."

"I hope you didn't get into an accident?"

"Miraculously, I did not. God protected me from harm, but he did something else that was far more miraculous. Through his Holy Spirit, God reached down into the very core of my being and washed away all my fears, doubts, and anxieties relative to my move to Houston. Sita, I was twenty-seven years old when that happened; come this May, I will have taught at

Houston Christian for twenty-seven years. That means I have spent fully half my life working at HCU. In all those years, I have never once doubted that God wanted me here."

"Didn't you say almost the same thing about your son not going to HCU?"

"What a great listener you are, Sita! You remind me of a character in an old movie of whom it is said that the way she listened was more eloquent than speech. In both instances—my going to Texas and Alex going to Michigan—God spoke to me in a way that caused me to weep those cathartic tears that cleanse the soul even more than they cleanse the eyes. Only God can draw out such tears, for they come from a wellspring that cannot be seen with the eyes or touched with the hands."

"Were those the only two times you cried like that?"

"There have been a few more times. May I share another?"

"Please do."

During the many hours I had been engaging in dialogue, my own discussions had not been the only ones going on around the table. Often, as I conversed with one or two people, the rest of the guests conducted their own simultaneous conversations. But now, I noticed, all eyes were on me. The Christian faith, as I had tried to demonstrate on that special Thanksgiving, is as logical, reasonable, and consistent as any other worldview system, but it is also more than that. At the heart of Christianity lies the personal testimony. It was not enough for me to explain and defend what Jesus did and said; I needed to share as well how he changed my life.

"My friends, once I secured my job at HCU, my wife and I began actively trying to have children. The process took three years and some divine intervention, but finally Alex was born in October 1994. His birth was a joyous answer to prayer, but it also marked the beginning of health issues that have plagued me ever since. Since my teens, I have been extremely allergic to cats and dogs, making it impossible for me to visit certain friends and relatives. Although I slowly learned to deal with that limitation, nothing prepared me for the chemical allergies that overwhelmed me about the time of Alex's birth. Only after much domestic strife and angst did we realize that the asthma attacks I kept getting were being caused by the perfume in Alex's diapers.

"Then my wife got pregnant again with Stacey, who was born in July 1996. This time we were careful to avoid all chemical scents, dyes, and cleaners. I looked forward to beginning our second stab at parenthood in a stress-free environment, but that was not to be. As my allergies to every type of chemical smell—from perfumes and colognes, to Lysol sprays and Glade sticks, to magic markers and scented lotions, to dry cleaning and plastic wrapping—escalated, I actually became allergic to Stacey. I could stand next to her with no reaction, but if I hugged her close to me, my asthma and headaches would come close to knocking me out."

"How terrible! How did you cope with it?"

"Even more than the physical debilitation, the emotional pain of not being able to hug my daughter was devastating. When I was watching the kids on the weekends, I would take them over to HCU so that my female students could hug Stacey—which they were always happy to do. But that did not take away my own aching sense of isolation or my fears that I was being prevented by illness from bonding fully with my daughter.

"Finally, about the time of Stacey's first birthday, I called out to God in all my confusion and agony. I felt like Ezekiel when God commanded him to cook his food over human dung. Ezekiel prayed God would allow him to avoid defilement by cooking over animal dung instead. In the spirit of Ezekiel, I told God that I could accept the chemical allergies if that was his will, but I begged him to heal me in relation to my daughter. God answered Ezekiel's request (Ezek 4:12-15), but he seemed to be deaf to my own."

"Were you ever healed?"

"That night, I switched the channel to Turner Classic Movies and watched Cecil B. DeMille's original silent-movie version of *The Ten Commandments*. Oddly, the director chose in his first stab at the biblical story to bookend his filming of the exodus out of Egypt with a modern morality tale. In the framing story, a man contracts leprosy, from which he is later miraculously cured. As I watched that scene, I knelt down on the ground and told God that I felt exactly like that leper—an outcast cut off from my own daughter. God did not respond to my cry of the heart, but after the movie ended, I felt compelled to do some channel surfing before shutting off the television.

"When I did that, I came upon a popular Bible teacher who was addressing a crowd on the exodus. The seeming coincidence grabbed my attention, and I began to listen to her more closely. Suddenly, and for no logical reason, she jumped from the exodus to talk about the man Jesus healed from leprosy. As far as I could tell, there was no thematic connection between the two stories, but when the connection was made, I fell to the ground and was overwhelmed by God's presence. As the Holy Spirit wrapped around me with an almost tangible embrace, those same tears that flooded out of me on my drive to Houston six years earlier returned with the power of a waterfall.

"Although the words were not audible, I heard God say to me that I was healed. Taking him at his word, I immediately walked over to the nursery, removed my shirt, lifted my sleeping daughter out of her crib, and hugged her to my chest. One hour later, I was still hugging her tightly. My allergic reaction was totally gone!"

"How wonderful! Did God heal you from your chemical allergies?"

"He did not. Though I could now hold Stacey close, all my other chemical allergies remained in full force—and have done so to this day. Since that time, I have become a speaker who travels widely around the country. As you can imagine, my chemical allergies have made traveling quite difficult for me, but God has used it to teach me humility. I'm a person who likes to be self-sufficient and organize things on my own. On account of my allergies, the Lord has forced me to ask for help and to rely on the charity of others to protect my health when I travel. That is to say, my allergies have taught me what Paul's thorn-in-the-flesh affliction taught him: that God's 'grace is sufficient for [me], for [his] power is made perfect in weakness' (2 Cor 12:9)."

As I finished speaking, I could see that my guests had been moved deeply by my story. Some even had tears in their eyes. Though I could not prove by scientific means that God had intervened and performed a miracle, they could discern the hand of an all-powerful, all-loving God in my story of brokenness and restored wholeness.

"My friends," I said, "we are not alone in a dark, uncaring universe, vainly trying to carve out fleeting moments of ecstasy while the cold, impersonal laws of nature drive us like so many cogs in a machine. No, we live in an open universe, alive with God's presence and love. Yes, that presence brings with it accountability, but it brings as well meaning and purpose and joy! And that is why the thing we are celebrating today is something that we should celebrate every day of the year: Thanksgiving!"

With that, a deep but palpable silence fell over all of us, so much so that we spent the next few minutes staring quietly into the slowly dying fire. As the last ember burned out, the lovely voice of my daughter rose up in the cool night air:

> Great is Thy faithfulness!
> Great is Thy faithfulness!
> Morning by morning new mercies I see.
> All I have needed Thy hand hath provided;
> Great is Thy faithfulness, Lord, unto me!

Then she walked over to me and gave me a crushing bear hug. A few moments later, Alex walked over and joined in the hug.

As we embraced in silence, everyone rose, put on their jackets, and returned to the house. All was the same, and yet all had changed. We had all, in our own way, been touched by the divine.

Thus ended the most memorable Thanksgiving of my life.

A NOTE TO THE READER

ALTHOUGH I DID HOST AN INTERNATIONAL POTLUCK at my home several Thanksgivings ago, something I have done for many years and continue to do today, the story you have read is fictional. Many of the things that happen in the story did happen on that day, and all the people in the dialogue are patterned after real people, sometimes in composite form, with whom I have dialogued over the last twenty-five years. The things that happen in the narrative did not happen on a single day, and the cast of characters were never all at my home at the same time. Still, the people are real, the conversations are real, and all the personal stories shared about myself, my children, my students, and my university are true. I have assembled all of them together in one place to illustrate how conversations about faith, miracles, and the meaning of life might play out with a diverse group of people from different ages, backgrounds, and religions. Houston International Christian Fellowship (HICF) is a real group with a powerful and long-lasting ministry, and it has been an honor and a privilege for me to be a part of it.

WHY EVERYONE IS SO POLITE IN THIS BOOK

A GUIDE TO ENGAGING WITH THE CONVERSATION

ALTHOUGH THE LEVEL OF POLITENESS AND RESPECT to which everyone adheres in the dialogue you have just read may seem unachievable in our modern, polarized world, I assure you it is not an impossible feat. Here are some tips I have learned over a lifetime of evangelism for defusing anger and defensiveness and promoting openness and the free exchange of ideas. I will use *we* here to refer to anyone who wants to break down barriers and communicate on a deeper level with spiritual seekers.

- Listening is as important as speaking. We must carefully discern what the real issue is that is holding a seeker back from faith. If our listening is too superficial, we will too quickly give a canned answer that does not address the real issue with which the person is struggling.
- We must avoid speaking always in black-and-white terms. Yes, there are true and false beliefs about God, but some wrong answers are closer to the truth than others. We must build a bridge rather than erect a wall. If we will remember that Christianity is the only *complete* truth, we will be able to find bits and pieces of truth in all other religions and cultures and use those bits and pieces as ways to connect with others on the big questions of life.
- We must do our homework. It is unwise to engage a Hindu, Buddhist, or Muslim in dialogue if we know nothing of their religion or culture (the two are often intimately intertwined, especially in non-Western cultures). That does not mean we have to be experts in world religions, but it does mean we need to know enough not to fall prey to

stereotypes about other religions. If you can quote their holy books, they will trust you more and so listen more carefully.

- We must offer as much praise and encouragement as we can. When appropriate, we must affirm seekers for being sincere in their desire to follow God and knowledgeable in their own religion or in the aspects of Christianity that are confusing them or holding them back. Let them feel safe to speak their mind because they know they will not be ridiculed or willfully misunderstood.
- We must ask questions that draw them out and help them to clarify their concerns. We must learn to see that their concerns are, at the same time, both like those of all other people on the planet and specific to their culture or religion. We must treat them as individuals who are also members of the human race.
- We must avoid jargon as much as we can and address the essential issues we all struggle with. Keep the focus on what C. S. Lewis called mere Christianity, the essential elements of the faith that all believing Christians share.
- We do not have to close the deal every time we share Christ with someone. It is not always our job to lead someone in that moment to confessing Christ as Lord. Often our job is to plant seeds or help water them. In the end, it is the Holy Spirit who does the reaping.
- We must remember the importance of building trust, especially with people from other religions who do not always feel understood by Americans. Often, they will not listen to our arguments for Jesus until they feel they can trust us as someone who respects and cares about them.
- We must show hospitality and be willing to share our own struggles and triumphs. The more we become a fellow pilgrim rather than a distant sage who knows all the answers, the more we will be trusted.
- Instead of leading people to the Lord and then getting them to join our fellowship, it is often a good idea to get them to join our fellowship first. If they see the reality of love and camaraderie in our group, they will be more open to hearing the secret of that camaraderie.

- We must not lose our tempers or ridicule other Christians or other seekers; such things cause people to shut down. We must gently take back the conversation if others fall into ridicule or overjudgmentalism.
- We must make clear that the God we are defending is the God of the Bible, not the God in whose name people commit acts that are inconsistent with Scripture. Of course, if we expect others to engage our God rather than a straw-man God, we must return that favor and allow them to articulate the God of their religion.
- We must be careful not to confuse the God of Scripture with our own cultural concerns and hangups. Let us make clear that Christ is the Savior of the world and not just of a particular people group.
- We must get to know the seekers we are sharing with as individuals and not as customers. We must make it clear in our words and our body language that we see them as friends regardless of whether they agree with us. We must show that we are sincerely concerned with them and want to learn from them about their own culture, religion, and personal struggles.
- Above all, we must avoid gotcha arguments that lure people into apologetical traps. Such tactics may allow us to win the argument, but we will lose the soul in the process. Apologetics is not a game. It is not about winning; it is about sharing Christ, clarifying the claims of the Bible, and building relationships.

FURTHER READING

Chapter One

Much of what I say in this chapter can be traced back to C. S. Lewis's 1947 classic, *Miracles* (HarperCollins, 2001). In this still timely book, Lewis explains why it is that miracles do not break the laws of nature and are not a violation of the dignity of God. He also explains that people who refuse, on the basis of their unproven worldview, to believe in the possibility of miracles will not accept a miracle even if it is performed in front of their eyes. Americans may think that seeing is believing, but Lewis shows that it is more often the case that believing is seeing. Anyone interested in the issues raised in this chapter must read this book, though please don't let yourself get bogged down in chapter three; if you find it difficult, just skip it and move on to chapter four.

If you would like some concrete, well-documented proof that miracles still happen in the modern world, please consult Craig Keener's two-volume *Miracles: The Credibility of the New Testament Accounts* (Baker, 2011). In addition to documenting the hundreds of miracles he describes, Keener rebuts the key arguments that have been made against miracles since the time of David Hume.

A good overall study is presented in R. Douglas Geivett and Gary R. Habermas's *In Defense of Miracles* (InterVarsity Press, 1997). I have also found chapter two of William Dembski's *Intelligent Design: The Bridge Between Science and Religion* (InterVarsity Press, 1999) and objection number two of Lee Strobel's *The Case for Faith* (Zondervan, 2000) to be quite helpful in framing the modern attack against miracles. Also see chapters one through three of my *Atheism on Trial* (Harvest, 2018) and chapter five of my *Apologetics for the 21st Century* (Crossway, 2010).

Chapter Two

For reading and studying the Qur'an, I like to use the translation of M. A. S. Abdel Haleem (Oxford World Classics, 2005). Abdel Haleem is a Muslim, and he works hard in his translation to make the Qur'an as accessible as possible. He softens things a bit—for example, he translates "fear of God" as "be mindful" of God, and uses *unbeliever* rather than *infidel*—but, out of fairness, I think it is right to allow a believer in the Qur'an to present it to a Western audience that has been exposed to much misinformation about the nature and teachings of Islam.

I think the best book for understanding Islam and Christianity is Nabeel Qureshi's very personal but also highly analytical *Seeking Allah, Finding Jesus: A Devout Muslim Encounters Christianity* (Zondervan, 2016). His *No God but One: Allah or Jesus? A Former Muslim Investigates the Evidence for Islam and Christianity* (Zondervan, 2016) is also excellent. For a single book that distinguishes the Christian worldview, not only from that of Islam but from secularism, Marxism, postmodernism, and new spirituality, see *Understanding the Times: A Survey of Worldviews*, by Jeff Myers and David Noebel (David C. Cook, 2015).

C. S. Lewis's liar-lunatic-Lord argument can be found in his greatest apologetics work, *Mere Christianity* (HarperCollins, 2001), though it was really Josh McDowell, in his highly influential *More than a Carpenter* (Tyndale, 1977), who framed the argument in that catchy, alliterative form. Speaking of Lewis, an excellent book that pits Lewis's apologetical arguments against the deism of John F. Kennedy and the Eastern mysticism of Aldous Huxley (all three of whom died on the same day) is Peter Kreeft's *Between Heaven and Hell* (InterVarsity Press, 1982). Kreeft conducts the argument in the form of a Socratic dialogue, a form he uses in a number of his other books. Kreeft is the modern master of the dialogue form, and this book owes a debt to him. Also see chapters three and seventeen of my *Apologetics for the 21st Century*.

A great resource for assessing the claims of Christ is part two of Lee Strobel's *The Case for Christ* (Zondervan, 1998). Josh McDowell's *The New Evidence That Demands a Verdict* (Thomas Nelson, 1999) documents in outline form how Jesus fulfilled the Old Testament prophecies of the Messiah.

The text of the *Gita* I prefer is *Bhagavad-Gita: The Song of God*, translated by Swami Prabhavananda and Christopher Isherwood (Marcel Rodd, 1944).

Chapter Three

The classic defense of the historical accuracy of the New Testament, one I consult often, is F. F. Bruce's *The New Testament Documents: Are They Reliable?* (InterVarsity Press, 1973). The most recent and most accessible defense is Craig Blomberg's *Can We Still Believe the Bible? An Evangelical Engagement with Contemporary Questions* (Brazos, 2014). Blomberg's *The Historical Reliability of the Gospels* (InterVarsity Press, 1987) is also well worth reading. Also see part one of Strobel's *The Case for Christ*.

Two accessible defenses of the historical accuracy of the Jesus presented in the Gospels are Gary Habermas's *The Historical Jesus* (College Press, 1996) and N. T. Wright's *Who Was Jesus?* (Eerdmans, 1992). For a scholarly but still accessible study of the eyewitness testimony on which the Gospels are based, see Richard Bauckham's *Jesus and the Eyewitnesses: The Gospels as Eyewitness Testimony* (Eerdmans, 2008). For a second scholarly but accessible work that establishes that the first-century church believed in the deity of Christ, see Larry Hurtado's *Lord Jesus Christ: Devotion to Jesus in Earliest Christianity* (Eerdmans, 2005).

For three refutations of the false claims made in Dan Brown's *Da Vinci Code*, see Darrell Bock's *Breaking the Da Vinci Code* (Thomas Nelson, 2004), Josh McDowell's *The Da Vinci Code: A Quest for Answers* (Green Key Books, 2006), and Lee Strobel and Garry Poole's *Exploring The Da Vinci Code* (Zondervan, 2006).

The passages I quote in this chapter from Clement and Ignatius are taken from *Early Christian Writings: The Apostolic Fathers*, translated by Maxwell Staniforth and revised by Andrew Louth (Penguin, 1987). Dorothy Sayers's *The Whimsical Christian* (Macmillan, 1978) argues, as I do here, that creeds do not invent orthodoxy but put them into philosophical form when the situation demands: See, in particular, "The Dogma Is the Drama," "What Do We Believe?," and "Creed or Chaos?" And make sure to check out Michael Licona's *Why Are There Differences in the Gospels? What We Can Learn from Ancient Biography* (Oxford University Press, 2016).

Finally, parts one and two of Kenneth Samples's *Without a Doubt: Answering the 20 Toughest Faith Questions* (Baker, 2004) offer incisive defenses and overviews of the reliability of the Gospels, the claims of Christ, the nature of the incarnation and Trinity, and the formation of the creeds.

In *Ancient Voices: An Insider's Look at the Early Church* (Stone Tower, 2022) I give the lie to the false argument that Christian theology was invented at Nicaea by surveying and quoting heavily from the early church fathers, martyrs, theologians, and heresy hunters of the second and third centuries. Also see chapters ten, sixteen, and twenty of my *Apologetics for the 21st Century*.

Chapter Four

Though I don't reference the book again, chapters fifteen and sixteen of Lewis's *Miracles* make a very helpful distinction between miracles of the old creation (turning water to wine and feeding the five thousand), which speed up natural processes, thus reminding us of the miracle that is already written into nature; and miracles of the new creation (resurrection and walking on water), which point ahead to what the world will be like in perfection.

For information on the complexity of DNA, see Francis Collins's *The Language of God: A Scientist Presents Evidence for Belief* (Free Press, 2006) and Stephen Meyer's *The Signature in the Cell: DNA and the Evidence for Intelligent Design* (HarperCollins, 2010). Collins headed the Human Genome Project, while Meyer is one of the leaders of the intelligent design movement.

The best place to start reading about the resurrection is part three of Strobel's *The Case for Christ*. My first encounter with the overwhelming evidence for the resurrection came from reading Frank Morison's *Who Moved the Stone* (Zondervan, 1958), written by a Strobel-like journalist who set out to disprove the resurrection and ended up believing it himself. For a fuller, highly readable presentation of the evidence, see Gary Habermas and Michael Licona's *The Case for the Resurrection of Jesus* (Kregel, 2004). For a more academic but still accessible study, see N. T. Wright's *The Resurrection of the Son of God* (Augsburg Fortress, 2003). Further evidence for the resurrection can be found in William Lane Craig's *The Son Rises: Historical Evidence for the Resurrection of Jesus* (Wipf & Stock, 2000).

Rudolf Bultmann's weighty *Theology of the New Testament* is available from Baylor University Press (2007). For a highly readable book that defends Christianity from claims that Jesus was a myth, see Rice Broocks's *Man, Myth, Messiah: Answering History's Greatest Question* (Thomas Nelson, 2016). For a fascinating study that uses modern forensics to establish the reliability of the Gospels and their presentation of Jesus and the resurrection, see J. Warner Wallace's *Cold-Case Christianity: A Homicide Detective Investigates the Claims of the Gospels* (David C. Cook, 2013). I would also highly recommend Norman Geisler and Frank Turek's *I Don't Have Enough Faith to Be an Atheist* (Crossway, 2004).

Also see chapters fourteen, eighteen, and twenty-two of my *Apologetics for the 21st Century.*

Chapter Five

In *The Unexpected Journey: Conversations with People Who Turned from Other Beliefs to Jesus* (Zondervan, 2005), Thom Rainer offers a series of interviews with Christians who converted to Christ both from traditional religions such as Islam, Judaism, and Hinduism and from less traditional ones such as New Age astrology and Satanism. The dialogue format of Rainer's book makes it a good complement to this book.

For an accessible overview of the life of the Buddha written by an American who gravitates toward New Age philosophy, see Deepak Chopra's *Buddha: A Story of Enlightenment* (HarperOne, 2008). Timothy Tennent's *Christianity at the Religious Roundtable: Evangelicalism in Conversation with Hinduism, Buddhism, and Islam* (Baker, 2002) is an excellent resource for those wishing to carry on the conversations begun in this book.

The role that desire plays in drawing us to God and heaven runs throughout the work of C. S. Lewis and is particularly prominent in his spiritual autobiography, *Surprised by Joy* (Harcourt Brace, 1966), and his allegorical telling of his road to faith, *The Pilgrim's Regress* (Eerdmans, 1981). His great sermon, "The Weight of Glory," is anthologized in *The Weight of Glory and Other Addresses* (Macmillan, 1980). Two other books that draw out the role of desire in the Christian life are John Eldredge's *The Journey of Desire: Searching for the Life We've Only Dreamed Of* (Thomas Nelson, 2000) and Peter Kreeft's *Heaven: The Heart's Deepest Longing* (Ignatius, 1989).

For Plato's teachings on reincarnation, see the "Myth of Er" at the end of the *Republic*. To read the collected writings of the various Gnostic sects, see *The Nag Hammadi Library*, edited by James M. Robinson (HarperCollins, 1990). For William Blake's Gnostic ideas, see chapter four of my *The Eye of the Beholder: How to See the World Like a Romantic Poet* (Winged Lion, 2011). Alister McGrath's *The Twilight of Atheism: The Rise and Fall of Disbelief in the Modern World* (Doubleday, 2004–2006) unpacks the negative legacy of the French Revolution.

Also see chapters eight through ten of my *Atheism on Trial*.

Chapter Six

It is most fortunate that an excellent book now exists that discusses the problem of gay marriage and transgenderism in terms of our nature as embodied souls. Nancy Pearcey's *Love Thy Body: Answering Hard Questions about Life and Sexuality* (Baker, 2018) is a must-read for anyone trying to navigate the LGBT challenge. It also connects the dots between LGBT issues on the one hand and abortion and euthanasia on the other. Another fine, irenic book on the subject is Sean McDowell and John Stonestreet's *Same-Sex Marriage: A Thoughtful Approach to God's Design for Marriage* (Baker, 2014).

M. Scott Peck's bestselling *The Road Less Traveled: A New Psychology of Love, Traditional Values and Spiritual Growth* (Touchstone, 1978) is worth reading in its entirety. The passage I quote appears on page 53. I would also highly recommend his *People of the Lie: The Human Hope for Healing Human Evil* (Touchstone, 1983), which makes the powerful argument that the heart of evil lies in an extreme form of narcissism.

The main source for information on the sexual practices of certain Gnostic sects is *The Panarion of Epiphanius of Salamis: Book I (Sects 1–46)*, volume 63 in the Nag Hammadi and Manichaean Studies series (SBL Press, 2016). This book can also be found free online. The best way, though, to get into the mind of Gnosticism, with its dualistic understanding of good and evil and its low view of the body and of matter, is to read books three through five of Saint Augustine's *Confessions* (Penguin, 1961).

Josh McDowell has written a number of pragmatic books to help equip parents to teach their children the value of abstinence. They may not be exciting to read in literary terms, but they lay out the facts effectively. I would suggest *Why True Love Waits: The Definitive Book on How to Help Your Kids Resist Sexual Pressure* (Tyndale, 2002).

Chapter Seven

The subject of the conquest of Canaan continues to cause much debate. The best current writer on the subject is Paul Copan, who has provided two books that offer much insight into the topic: *Is God a Moral Monster? Making Sense of the Old Testament God* (Baker, 2011); *Did God Really Command Genocide? Coming to Terms with the Justice of God* (Baker, 2014). Another fine book that takes up the same controversial subject is David Lamb's *God Behaving Badly: Is the God of the Old Testament Angry, Sexist and Racist*? (InterVarsity Press, 2011). A classic study that takes up this difficult topic, alongside the wider issues of hell and the problem of pain, is John Wenham's *The Goodness of God* (InterVarsity Press, 1974).

Also see chapter six of my *Atheism on Trial*, where I rebut, with the help of Tertullian, an early church heretic named Marcion who sought to throw out the Old Testament and its supposed God of wrath.

Chapter Eight

Throughout the third section of this book (chaps. 7–9), I make reference to some of my favorite passages in the works of C. S. Lewis. For his argument that God and heaven are greater, not less, than man and earth, see chapters eleven and sixteen of *Miracles*. For his Augustinian description of the Trinity and what it means to participate in the life of the Trinity, see *Mere Christianity* 4.2-4. For his argument that religion arose out of a sense of the numinous that is unique to man, see chapter one of *The Problem of Pain* (HarperCollins, 2001). For his argument that it is finally we who choose hell and for his suggestion that a person might still have a chance to accept Christ after his death, see chapter eight of *The Problem of Pain*, chapter nine of *The Great Divorce* (HarperCollins, 2001), and chapter fifteen of *The Last Battle* (Collier, 1970). For his discussion that Christ was the myth made fact, see "Myth Became Fact," in *God in the Dock* (Eerdmans, 1970). For his thoughts on joy (*Sehnsucht*), see chapter one of his spiritual autobiography, *Surprised by Joy* (HarperOne, 2017); all of his allegorical autobiography, *The Pilgrim's Regress* (Eerdmans, 2014); and *Mere Christianity* 3.10.

A powerful but irenic defense of Christ as the only way to God can be found in James Edwards's *Is Jesus the Only Savior?* (Eerdmans, 2005). Lesslie Newbigin's *The Gospel in a Pluralist Society* (Eerdmans, 1989) shows that true Christianity is neither imperialistic nor antipluralistic. For those who find Christianity to be too exclusivist and narrow, James Choung's *True Story: A Christianity Worth Believing In* (InterVarsity Press, 2008) offers a fuller vision of the gospel. Timothy Keller's *The Reason for God: Belief in an Age of Skepticism* (Dutton, 2008) takes up powerfully new atheist critiques of the so-called exclusivity of Christianity.

Also see my reading lists for chapters two and five of this book, chapter nineteen of my *Apologetics for the 21st Century*, and chapter six of my *Lewis Agonistes: How C. S. Lewis Can Train Us to Wrestle with the Modern and Postmodern World* (B&H, 2003).

Chapter Nine

In addition to the C. S. Lewis books listed above, I have enjoyed a number of other books that take up the role of desire in a person's journey to God: Brent Curtis and John Eldredge's *The Sacred Romance: Drawing Closer to the Heart of God* (Thomas Nelson, 1997), John Eldredge's *The Journey of Desire: Searching for the Life We Only Dreamed Of* (Thomas Nelson, 2000), Peter Kreeft's *Heaven: The Heart's Deepest Longing* (Ignatius, 1989), and Alister McGrath's *The Unknown God: Searching for Spiritual Fulfillment* (Eerdmans, 1999). Above all, read Don Richardson's *Eternity in Their Hearts* (Regal, 1984), which documents how tribal groups across the world have preserved a belief in the one true God even in the midst of animism.

Also see chapter three of *Lewis Agonistes* and the introduction and conclusion to my *From Achilles to Christ: Why Christians Should Read the Pagan Classics* (InterVarsity Press, 2007).

Chapter Ten

For a classic study of New Age spirituality, see Bob Larson's *Straight Answers on the New Age* (Thomas Nelson, 1989). For Charles Taylor's discussion of how the traditional view of a porous universe gave way to the modern buffered self, see chapter fifteen of his *A Secular Age* (Belknap, 2007). For the memoir of a woman who came out of the New Age into Christian belief, see Doreen Virtue's *Deceived No More: How Jesus Led Me Out of the New Age and into His Word* (Thomas Nelson, 2020).

For a positive view of meditative prayer that stays, I believe, within the bounds of orthodoxy, see Thomas Keating's *Intimacy with God: An Introduction to Centering Prayer* (Crossroad, 2009). For positive views of Celtic spirituality, see Balzer Tracy's *Thin Places: An Evangelical Journey into Celtic Christianity* (Leafwood, 2007) and Esther De Waal's *The Celtic Way of Prayer: The Recovery of the Religious Imagination* (PRH Christian, 1998). For the Jesus Prayer, see *The Way of a Pilgrim*, by an anonymous medieval Russian monk, translated by Nina A. Toumanova (Dover, 2008). Also see *Practicing the Presence of God*, by a humble seventeenth-century Parisian monastery cook named Brother Lawrence (Whitaker, 1982). For a good anthology of Christian mystics who often have an Eastern bent, see *The Essential Writings of Christian Mysticism*, edited by Bernard McGinn (Modern Library, 2006).

In chapter three of *Lewis Agonistes* ("Wrestling with the New Age"), I argue that C. S. Lewis can help us reach modern people hungry for mystery and connection. In *The Myth Made Fact: Reading Greek and Roman Mythology Through Christian Eyes* (Classical Academic Press, 2020), I find true wisdom in ancient myths, arguing, in chapters eleven and twenty-five, for a valid distinction between black magic and white magic.

Chapter Eleven

One of my favorite apologists is Francis Schaeffer, a man who ministered to a generation of hippies who longed for intimacy and authenticity but saw in the God of the church only a distant and authoritarian figure cut off from their deepest desires. In *He Is There and He Is Not Silent* (Tyndale, 1985), Schaeffer argues for a personal, trinitarian God who speaks and who would be known.

G. K. Chesterton's *Orthodoxy: The Romance of Faith* (Image Books, 1959) does a wonderful job conjuring for us an active, dynamic God who is involved in every aspect of our lives and whose personhood can be seen even in the so-called clockwork universe of Newton. Also see Chesterton's *Everlasting Man* (Image Books, 1955) for a breezy but incisive reading of history that locates God's hand working in the details.

For two very different books that capture to the full the dynamism of the Christian faith and its triune God, see Thomas Howard's *Christ the Tiger* (Ignatius, 1990) and John Piper's *Desiring God: Meditations of a Christian Hedonist* (Multnomah, 2003).

Chapter Twelve

The best place to start is with C. S. Lewis *The Problem of Pain*. After that, I would suggest Peter Kreeft's *Making Sense Out of Suffering* (Servant, 1986), Philip Yancey's *Where Is God When It Hurts* (Zondervan, 1990), Joni Eareckson Tada's *When God Weeps* (Zondervan, 2000), Randy Alcorn's *If God Is Good: Faith in the Midst of Suffering and Evil* (Multnomah, 2014), and objection number one of Lee Strobel's *Case for Faith*.

Also see chapters four and fifteen of my *Apologetics for the 21st Century*, chapter eight of my *Atheism on Trial*, and chapter four of my *Lewis Agonistes*.

Chapter Thirteen

For three classic spiritual autobiographies that are as similar as they are different and that celebrate God's provision in times of difficulty and darkness, see Augustine's *Confessions*, John Bunyan's *Grace Abounding to the Chief of Sinners* (CreateSpace, 2015), and C. S. Lewis's *Surprised by Joy*.

ALSO BY THE AUTHOR

From Plato to Christ
978-0-8308-5304-5

From Aristotle to Christ
978-1-5140-1132-4

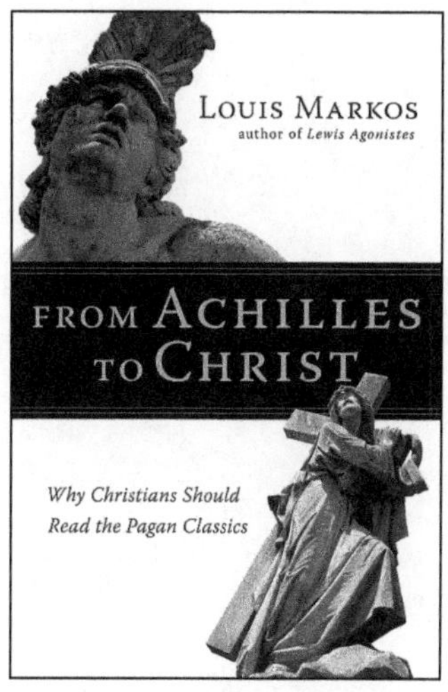

From Achilles to Christ
978-0-8308-2593-6

Passing the Torch
978-1-5140-1130-0